THE **LIFE** HISTORY OF THE UNITED STATES

Volume 8: 1890-1901

REACHING FOR EMPIRE

TIME
LIFE
BOOKS ®

THE TIME-LIFE LIBRARY OF BOATING

HUMAN BEHAVIOR

THE ART OF SEWING

THE OLD WEST

THE EMERGENCE OF MAN

THE AMERICAN WILDERNESS

THE TIME-LIFE ENCYCLOPEDIA OF GARDENING

LIFE LIBRARY OF PHOTOGRAPHY

THIS FABULOUS CENTURY

FOODS OF THE WORLD

TIME-LIFE LIBRARY OF AMERICA

TIME-LIFE LIBRARY OF ART

GREAT AGES OF MAN

LIFE SCIENCE LIBRARY

THE LIFE HISTORY OF THE UNITED STATES

TIME READING PROGRAM

LIFE NATURE LIBRARY

LIFE WORLD LIBRARY

FAMILY LIBRARY:

   HOW THINGS WORK IN YOUR HOME

   THE TIME-LIFE BOOK OF THE FAMILY CAR

   THE TIME-LIFE FAMILY LEGAL GUIDE

   THE TIME-LIFE BOOK OF FAMILY FINANCE

THE **LIFE** HISTORY OF THE UNITED STATES

Consulting Editor, Henry F. Graff

Volume 8: 1890-1901

REACHING FOR EMPIRE

by Bernard A. Weisberger

and the Editors of

TIME-LIFE BOOKS

TIME-LIFE BOOKS, NEW YORK

TIME-LIFE BOOKS

FOUNDER: Henry R. Luce 1898-1967

Editor-in-Chief: Hedley Donovan
Chairman of the Board: Andrew Heiskell
President: James R. Shepley

Vice Chairman: Roy E. Larsen

MANAGING EDITOR: Jerry Korn
Assistant Managing Editors: Ezra Bowen,
David Maness, Martin Mann, A. B. C. Whipple
Planning Director: Oliver E. Allen
Art Director: Sheldon Cotler
Chief of Research: Beatrice T. Dobie
Director of Photography: Melvin L. Scott
Senior Text Editors: Diana Hirsh, William Frankel
Assistant Planning Director: Carlotta Kerwin
Assistant Art Director: Arnold C. Holeywell
Assistant Chief of Research: Myra Mangan

PUBLISHER: Joan D. Manley
General Manager: John D. McSweeney
Business Manager: John Steven Maxwell
Sales Director: Carl G. Jaeger
Promotion Director: Paul R. Stewart
Public Relations Director: Nicholas Benton

THE LIFE HISTORY OF THE UNITED STATES
Editorial Staff for Volume 8
EDITOR: Sam Welles
Assistant Editor: Harold C. Field
Designer: Douglas R. Steinbauer
Staff Writers: Gerald Simons, Jon Swan,
Edmund White
Chief Researcher: Clara E. Nicolai
Researchers: Natalia Zunino, Mary Youatt,
Ellen Leiman, Ruth Silva, Evelyn Hauptman,
Jean Snow, Barbara Moir, Malabar Brodeur,
Elizabeth Collins, Lilla Zabriskie,
Patricia Tolles, Joan Scafarello

EDITORIAL PRODUCTION
Production Editor: Douglas B. Graham
Assistant Production Editors:
Gennaro C. Esposito, Feliciano Madrid
Quality Director: Robert L. Young
Assistant Quality Director: James J. Cox
Associate: Serafino J. Cambareri
Copy Staff: Eleanore W. Karsten (chief),
Ann Lang, Gail Weesner, Florence Keith,
Pearl Sverdlin
Picture Department: Dolores A. Littles
Art Assistants: James D. Smith, Wayne R. Young

THE AUTHOR of Volumes 7 and 8 in this series, Bernard A. Weisberger, has concentrated on the study of the United States from the complex Civil War period through the early 20th Century. His wide familiarity with the social and literary history of those years is reflected in his works, which include 11 books, among them *Reporters for the Union, They Gathered at the River, The American Newspaperman, The American Heritage History of the American People* and a number of essays and articles in professional journals. Born in Hudson, New York, Dr. Weisberger studied at Columbia University and the University of Chicago and was Professor of History at the University of Rochester. He is currently Visiting Professor of History at Vassar College and a contributing editor to *American Heritage.*

THE CONSULTING EDITOR for this series, Henry F. Graff, is Professor of History at Columbia University in New York.

Valuable assistance in preparing this volume was given by Roger Butterfield, who served as picture consultant: photographers Eliot Elisofon and Dmitri Kessel; Editorial Production, Norman Airey; Library, Benjamin Lightman; Picture Collection, Doris O'Neil; Photographic Laboratory, George Karas; TIME-LIFE News Service, Murray J. Gart. Revisions Staff: Harold C. Field, Joan Chambers.

CONTENTS

1. THE THRUST
OF NEW IDEAS

As industrialism worked its changes in American society in the quarter century after the Civil War, it left visible evidence of its progress on the very face of the land. By 1890 an observer could see the modern world in such things as electric lights gleaming on asphalt-paved streets, or oil-laden barges chuffing down a river where birchbark canoes had ridden high and light less than a lifetime ago. Less visible were other alterations, no less portentous. The intellectual foundations which supported American life were changing, and some of them were disappearing as surely as the buffalo.

The average citizen, however, believed that his social order was the world's best and his political system its wisest. The growth of the United States under freedom was proof of this, and the preservation of the nation from disunion in 1861-1865 reinforced that proof (to Northerners, in any case). The future would be ever richer, more spacious for each new generation.

This tight, comfortable little cosmos was founded on revealed religion, natural law, common sense and idealism. God had chosen the American people and made them the special custodians of His moral truths. The natural universe ran on timeless and regular principles. Man could comprehend them, and in applying them to practical problems had created awesome new mechanical servants. The onward march of the mind was matched by a growing purification of life, for each man had in him a spark of divine purpose.

It was all put very well in a novel published in 1867 by John W. De Forest,

ASSAYING GOLD, Thomas Price represents the practical, productive technicians from whose laboratories came so many new processes of value to late 19th Century America.

Herbert Spencer, the "Watch-dog of Science," views the attempts by members of "The Society for the Suppression of Blasphemous Literature" to muzzle his radical ideas. However, he never lost his composure. When a friend commented that Spencer's brow stayed unlined despite the demanding thinking he did, the savant said, "I suppose it is because I am never puzzled."

a New England veteran of the Civil War, who had one of his characters observe that slavery must be gotten out of the way "like any other obstacle to the progress of humanity. It must make room for something more consonant with the railroad, electric-telegraph, printing-press, inductive philosophy, and practical Christianity." There was a good deal of inconsistency in this valiantly optimistic creed, but it was well fitted to a bustling and growing country in the half century before the Civil War.

Postwar intellectual developments gave these concepts a hard buffeting. It had been possible to tame the older, scientific skepticism of the 18th Century and reconcile it with piety and hopefulness. But now, suddenly, science was asserting that man was simply a high-class animal, a form of life, and that all forms of life were constantly changing in response to inexorable laws. There was no longer Man, or Mankind; there were only men, differing from time to time and place to place as did cattle or trees.

THE villain in the piece—or the hero, depending on individual preference— was Charles Darwin, the Englishman whose *Origin of Species,* published in 1859, set forth the doctrine of "natural selection." Darwin had studied the work of the English economist Thomas Malthus, which concluded that since plants and animals have the capacity to multiply in geometric ratio, many more are born than can possibly find food and living space; many must, therefore, die before maturing and propagating. There is consequently a struggle for existence in nature.

Proceeding from this point, Darwin reasoned that within any species, there are individual animals or plants which differ slightly, and without clear reason, from each other; some have characteristics which enable them to live in their environments, while others perish. The surviving individuals pass these characteristics on to their offspring. Like a successful farmer who mates his fattest sheep or strongest horses until an improved breed is created, so nature itself picks and sorts among multitudes of living creatures over millions of years, changing old species, creating new ones and eliminating others. Darwin called this process natural selection. The crude, shorthand formula for stating this electrifying theory of evolutionary change through natural selection was a four-word catch phrase: survival of the fittest.

It was not Charles Darwin who coined the phrase always associated with his name, but Herbert Spencer, an English philosopher with an encyclopedic mind and the tidy instincts of an engineer (which he had been). In the early '50s, Spencer was already developing the idea that the struggle for survival was a stimulus to human advance. When his work *Synthetic Philosophy* later appeared, its attempt to unify all human knowledge in the light of the struggle for survival brought him extraordinary acclaim in the United States. In good part this was due to the labors of a number of disciples, most notably a widely read, prolific scholar-at-large named John Fiske.

Fiske was only 18 when he discovered Spencer's works, which evoked in the young man worshipful admiration. By the time Fiske and other Spencerians and Darwinians were through adapting the master to American tastes, however, they had worked some curious changes in the original texts.

Some discussion of Spencer's ideas is indispensable to an understanding of his hold on the American mind. Spencer taught that the evolutionary processes of struggle, survival and selection were applicable to human institutions, too. The same general law which explained the disappearance of the dinosaur and the appearance of the long neck of the giraffe could also explain the emergence of the institutions of modern capitalism.

The laws of social development, said Spencer, were immutable and not to be tampered with except at the peril of the land that tried to interfere with the inscrutable ways by which "fit" institutions and individuals thrived and reproduced themselves. Moreover, the free and civilized individual was a highly complex and specialized product of the evolutionary process, which always tended from the simple toward the complex, from the homogeneous toward the heterogeneous. Historically, the direction had always been from the simple pagan, indistinguishable from his superstitious fellow tribesmen, to a marvel of individual tastes, choices, habits and perceptions—like, say, Herbert Spencer. It was essential to the untrammeled working of evolution that the freedom of this individual be safeguarded against the group.

It was the task of the state, in fact, to observe the struggle without hindering the strong or assisting the weak, interceding only to protect individual freedom from assault by others. Spencer thus became, from the early volumes of his *Synthetic Philosophy* until his death in 1903, the archprophet of *laissez faire*, the theory that a state should do absolutely nothing that could conceivably be done by individual effort. He even opposed public schools and postal service. This was sweet music to the many Americans who had long been willing to admire and encourage the rugged individualist.

On the other hand, Spencer held that metaphysics and theology were fields in which learning could only come to a dead end. Much could be learned by observation and comparison of various states of matter and energy, but once speculation turned to such questions as what first cause had created matter and energy, it became a profitless quest for the "Unknowable."

THIS view of Spencer's was somewhat arid for most Americans, reared in a tradition of belief in a Higher Power that took care of them. Fiske, among others, rectified the omission. Although he had stopped believing in the God of his New England ancestors before his freshman year at Harvard, he could not dismiss Him as airily as had Spencer. The slow process of mutation in time, he decided, was part of "the orderly manifestations of a Divine Power."

What was more, Fiske said, man was not merely a species of animal who would have his brief hour. Man was still the chief end of creation; indeed, "in the deadly struggle for existence which has raged through aeons of time," Fiske wrote, "the whole creation has been groaning and travailing together in order to bring forth that last consummate specimen of God's handiwork, the Human Soul." With God and the soul restored, evolution was acceptable to the spiritual descendants of Cotton Mather and Ralph Waldo Emerson.

Through dozens of lectures, encyclopedia articles and volumes on everything from archeology to zoology, Fiske and others popularized this version of a Spencerized "social Darwinism." Its impact was so wide that it is impossible to follow it everywhere. Certain articulate spokesmen for business took to Darwinism with glee, for it was obvious that if nature allowed only the fit to survive, then likewise the firms which outlasted their enemies in the jungle of competition were the chosen of evolution.

Andrew Carnegie, whose mind and pen were nimbler than those of most magnates, almost made a second career of expressing this philosophy publicly.

Charles Darwin thought his great abilities modest, but hoped that his writings would be of general interest. He was shocked that his theory was used to justify a ruthless philosophy. A colleague said of him, "There is a marvellous dumb sagacity about him—like that of a sort of miraculous dog—and he gets to the truth by ways as dark as those of the Heathen Chinee."

"The price which society pays for the law of competition" was great but unavoidable, he declared in 1889. "While the law may be sometimes hard for the individual, it is best for the race, because it insures the survival of the fittest in every department. We accept and welcome, therefore . . . the concentration of business, industrial and commercial, in the hands of a few . . . as being not only beneficial, but essential to the future progress of the race." And what of brotherhood and co-operation as a desirable alternative to competition? "This is not evolution, but revolution," said the steelmaker. "It necessitates the changing of human nature itself—a work of eons, even if it were good to change it, which we cannot know."

And what of obligations to the fallen in the struggle for existence? To Carnegie, "One of the serious obstacles to the improvement of our race is indiscriminate charity. It were better for mankind that the millions of the rich were thrown into the sea than so spent as to encourage the slothful, the drunken, the unworthy." True charity, he felt, meant giving "to help those who will help themselves." Appropriately enough, Carnegie called his beliefs "the gospel of wealth," a doctrine whose most striking aspect was its cheerful assumption that "our wonderful material development" inevitably brought "improved conditions in its train." To Carnegie the civilization which produced his steelworks was the flower of evolution.

Carnegie's views, adopted by lecturers, expounded by editors and politicians, became those of an entire generation. For these men, any attempt to change the *status quo* had to be fought. So they resisted the abolition of the gold standard, the adoption of women's suffrage, or the providing of public assistance in any form to farmers, workers, immigrants, the unemployed or the "weak." As William Graham Sumner, another Spencerian, wrote in 1883, improvement in social conditions would come only "by growth, never in the world by any reconstruction of society on the plan of some enthusiastic social architect. . . . Society needs first of all to be free from these meddlers."

Though men of the market place, and even professors and lecturers, might embrace evolution, the churches were put to some strain. Darwin's ideas on the origins of mankind left little room for Adam (not to mention the cargo of Noah's Ark). And without Adam, where was God? Where the Fall? Where the Redemption? Where theology altogether?

Particularly for those American church denominations which believed in the Bible without qualification, Darwinism was simply one more burden to bear. New discoveries in archeology and the scientific study of ancient and modern languages had already suggested that the Bible was not to be accepted word for word. In rural parsonages, there was suspicion of a higher Biblical criticism which rested on research done in German universities. Modernism was the fighting word used to describe all the unseen forces which were sweeping away a secure old world.

Yet the very appeal of a modern viewpoint was that it satisfied Americans yearning to be up-to-date. The scientific findings of the '80s therefore led some Americans to forswear traditional religion altogether, some to marry religion and science, and some to dress up the old-time faith in modern trappings. Three Americans of the '70s and '80s, Robert Ingersoll, Henry Ward Beecher and Dwight L. Moody, typified the various reactions.

"Royal Bob" Ingersoll, born in 1833, was the son of a Congregational minis-

"The Modern Theory of the Descent of Man" is an early American attempt to diagram evolution. In England William Gilbert wryly commented on the new theory: "Darwinian Man, though well-behaved, / At best is only a monkey shaved." American clergymen were far more distressed by Darwin's theory, and there was much "fluttering of . . . theologic nerves."

10

ter. He settled in Illinois, studied law, fought in the Civil War and became a Republican. In these respects his biography could be duplicated a hundred times in his generation. But Ingersoll was unusual in one respect. In his young manhood he had repudiated the formal religion of his father and became a dedicated anticlerical. In lecture after lecture he flailed away at the inconsistencies of the Biblical chronology, the miracles which defied common sense, the "immorality" and "chicanery" of the patriarchs. Above all, he excoriated clerical leaders—from pre-Reformation times of stake and fagot down to heresy-hunting contemporaries who, in his view, tried to obscure the light of scientific reason in the clouds of intolerance. His choicest barbs were reserved for the fear-inspiring, guilt-producing Hell of traditional Calvinist upbringing.

Gazing at a lush Standard Oil bloom, John D. Rockefeller coolly inspects a rival business he has nipped in the bud with the shears of competition. The skulls of other rivals lie at his feet. This cartoon is based on his son John D. Jr.'s statement: "The American Beauty rose can be produced in all its splendor only by sacrificing the early buds that grow up around it."

YET Ingersoll was not without a faith. "Reason, Observation and Experience—the Holy Trinity of Science—have taught us that happiness is the only good." This was his creed. The implicit hopefulness of this creed was what made Ingersoll typical of his time and place. In all respects save religious orthodoxy he was the epitome of Americanism: a lover of the flag, of motherhood and the Republican party. His oratory was employed in the service of many leading politicos of the Gilded Age, chiefly James G. Blaine, for whom he coined the wholly inappropriate name of "The Plumed Knight." His legal talents brought him wealth in the service of the high-riding and confident business interests of the expanding nation. But he was also a partisan of labor and the underdog. No wonder that in spite of steady assault from various pulpits he remained a well-loved figure to many men of his generation.

Fully 20 years older than Ingersoll was Henry Ward Beecher, who progressed from an unhappy childhood in New England parsonages to a spectacularly successful career as a preacher. He was one of 13 children (including Harriet Beecher Stowe) born to Lyman Beecher, himself a bustling and active American Presbyterian patriarch, whose love for his offspring was genuine, but who also clamped their lives in a kind of benevolent slavery.

More or less forced into the ministry by his father, Henry Ward Beecher found that he had a gift for poetic speech and a warm, outgoing nature that emphasized the redemptive side of Christian teaching and sidestepped theological problems and dark places. By the 1870s he had been for a quarter of a century the renowned pastor of Plymouth Congregational Church in Brooklyn, New York. The church was a thoroughly fashionable place to which the town's prosperous citizens came on Sundays to learn of their obligations to the Lord and vice versa. Beecher told them that they were loved. What was more, he added that they need not fear, for the God of their Sunday-school lessons and the God of evolution and the dynamo were one and the same.

"Science," Beecher asserted, "is but the deciphering of God's thought as revealed in the structure of this world." God had labored to prepare the globe as man's dwelling place; who could fail to marvel when he reflected on God's "compassionate waiting and working through illimitable ages and periods, compared with which a million years as marked by the clock are but seconds"? Scientific study, Beecher predicted, would "change theology, but only to bring out the simple temple of God in clearer and more beautiful lines and proportions." The great dualism between natural and revealed religion would end as man's "physical" and "spiritual" qualities were seen to come from the one source, God, and the unprejudiced Christian believer in science could proclaim to the church, "Rise, shine; Thy light has come."

While the portly, ruddy-faced pastor of Plymouth Church, his gray hair flowing down over his collar, was thus harmonizing Darwin and Genesis, another thickset son of New England was preaching a different set of ideas to the multitudes. This was Dwight Lyman Moody, born in western Massachusetts in 1837. As a youngster, he had gone from the countryside to the city of Boston. In 1856 he left New England for the challenging Midwestern atmosphere of booming Chicago. Moody originally intended to be a businessman, and had he stuck to his intention he certainly would have become a giant of commerce and industry. His big, over-200-pound frame was charged with incredible energy, and his mind not only mastered infinite quantities of detail but was wholly and lovingly absorbed in work, followed by more work and alternated with refreshing stretches of still more work.

YET God had not decreed that D. L. Moody should be a great merchant or manufacturer. In his youth he had "gotten religion." In Chicago he became a tireless lay worker, organizing and financing a Sunday school among slum children. Then in 1861 he abandoned his successful career as a traveling shoe salesman to give his full time to religion. He was very active in the Chicago Y.M.C.A. He surmounted a fire that burned out his first nondenominational church to build a second, and preached in both of them, though he was never ordained. He was without a peer at fund raising and staff recruitment. All his efforts were devoted to the work of getting more people back to the church from which the modern world was luring them. In leaving the world of commerce, it might be said that he gave up one kind of business. His new business was "saving" souls.

Moody was a fervent believer in the literal truth of the Biblical message. And he was convinced that once this simple message was conveyed to people, they would certainly dedicate themselves to living a Christian life. To Moody, there was no conflict between a Christian life and success in 19th Century America. Armed with this faith and his organizing powers, Moody became, beginning about 1875, the most successful evangelist seen up to that date. To thousands, packed into huge, gaslit arenas in New York, Brooklyn, Boston, Philadelphia, Chicago, Richmond, St. Louis—all the rising new cities and many of the old ones—he preached short, pungent sermons, in a quick, crisp, New England accent, free of all theological and dogmatic flourishes.

"He has the air of a businessman to whom time is extremely valuable," one reporter observed. In businesslike fashion, Moody told stories of wandering sheep and wayworn lads, of gray-haired mothers and weather-beaten fathers, of homes broken and hearts harrowed—and always, at the end, of the return of the prodigal and parental forgiveness. And he illustrated his single point—that God, too, was a loving and forgiving Father—with stories taken from the Bible, whose characters suddenly became recognizable contemporaries, speaking the common talk of the 1870s and organizing prayer meetings, making business trips or being tempted by saloons and circus shows. Along with Moody's sermons went melting little songs ("Rescue the Perishing," "Come Home, O Prodigal Child," "Ninety and Nine") played on a small organ and tenderly sung by Ira D. Sankey, his corpulent, bald and moustached musician-in-chief.

By such tactics, Moody did win multitudes for Christ. Moody's religion

Although clergyman Henry Ward Beecher had studied and avidly accepted the new theory of evolution, his busy life of preaching left him little time for careful reading. "One does not read a book through," he once said. "You read a book as you eat a fish . . . cut off the fins, take out the backbone, and there is a little meat left which you eat because it nourishes you."

had room only for the most literal interpretation of the Bible. He simply brushed aside doubts. He saw nothing that a botanist could tell him about the rose of Sharon, or a geologist about the Rock of Ages. No intellectual problems stood in the way of full acceptance of the gospel. It was a matter of simple and quick decision. "Who'll take Christ now?" Moody would urge a wavering audience. "That's all you want. With Christ you have eternal life and everything else you need. Without Him you must perish. He offers Himself to you. Who'll take Him?"

Dispensing such a simple, fundamental, Bible-centered faith in massive doses, Moody seemed a throwback to an earlier time. Yet it is worth noting that Moody was as modern in technique as he was old-fashioned in message. His "campaigns" were small masterpieces of organization. Posters, newspaper stories and handbills announced his schedule. Committees were organized, in advance of his appearance, to train and drill ushers, singers, assistants and special counselors. Money, contributed by successful Christian businessmen, was spent in large quantities, as was suitable in an era when men invested grandiosely to achieve massive results.

Moody's powers of setting things in motion were also employed in the creation of schools and leadership conferences, and for them he could always raise funds from the business giants of his generation, because, as one donor put it, "he is one of us." All of this made Moody a man of his time, confident that all problems could be solved by righteousness and elbow grease. In his own conservative way, he had made an up-to-date religious adjustment to the new, industrial way of life. Like Ingersoll, like Beecher, Moody stands out as a big man, confident in his own strength, his time and his nation—an example of the power of American popular thought to draw strength from the challenge of new ideas in the expansive post-Civil War days.

JUST as American churchmen refused to permit God to be banned from the new universe revealed by science and the machine, so America's professional scholars refused to give up the national faith in purposeful activity and self-improvement. This faith in self-perfection was at odds with the thinking of some of Darwin's and Spencer's disciples who extolled determinism, the philosophy that whatever befalls man is fixed in nature and beyond his control. But determinism was too much for 19th Century Americans to swallow, even when it was temptingly labeled "modernity." Americans had spent considerable effort to unburden themselves of the remnants of Puritan determinism, the doctrine that predestined man, regardless of individual merit, to glory or hell-fire. The idea of predestination had not suited a people who were so clearly, and in general so successfully, moving ahead. For the same reason, Americans were not likely for long to permit themselves to be regimented by Spencerian determinism after escaping the bonds of John Calvin's theology. By the 1880s new voices were being raised in defense of the proposition that evolutionary studies made man even more responsible for his destiny than he had been before the 19th Century.

Many of these new viewpoints were expressed by professors who specialized in a relatively new area, graduate study. The term was indicative of the growing pains then being felt by universities. There was a great expansion of knowledge, particularly in the sciences. Higher education began to go beyond the traditional four years of recitations, themes, translations, debates,

"Are you a Christian?" Dwight L. Moody asks a revival meeting in New York. The evangelist put this question to anyone, anywhere and at any time, until it became his trade-mark. Moody, it is said, stopped a stranger with his question, and the man replied, "It's none of your business." "Oh, yes it is," the preacher said. "Then you must be Moody," the man replied.

hazing and high jinks. After the Civil War, faculties of medicine and law in older centers of learning had become better organized and adopted higher standards. Moreover, facilities for postcollege study in areas outside medicine, law and theology started to appear.

In 1861, Yale conferred the first American degree of Doctor of Philosophy (Ph.D.). Harvard created a graduate school in 1872, and in 1876 Johns Hopkins University opened its doors in Baltimore. Most of the Hopkins faculty had been trained in German universities, then at the zenith of their reputation for promoting new research (and awarding advanced degrees) in the natural and biological sciences, linguistics, law, philosophy, comparative government, economics and many other subjects whose very names were strange to American academic life. Hopkins soon became a superb graduate school, sending forth young men in proud possession of the new and foreign-sounding doctorate in philosophy. Among them were a political scientist named Woodrow Wilson, a philosopher and future educator named John Dewey and a stream of others who would one day direct hospitals, make laws, sit in embassies and presidential Cabinets, and lead still other universities in the spirit of the new age.

Other new universities rose during this period: Cornell opened its doors in 1868, Stanford in 1891 and the University of Chicago (financed by John D. Rockefeller) in 1892. In them, as in older centers like Columbia, Princeton, Pennsylvania, in the state universities of the old Midwest such as Wisconsin and Michigan, and in the new tax-supported universities rising in the Plains and Rocky Mountain states, a great change was under way. For in place of the older methods of training by practical experience, the universities now provided professional and advanced training in mining, engineering, public health, education and related fields. Research crowded rote learning to the side. Inquiry in seminar and laboratory, rather than the transmission of established verities, became the business of a teacher.

IT was in such an atmosphere that scientific ideas were harnessed to optimism and activity. A few names chosen almost at random can suggest the depth, intensity and duration of the intellectual drives which everywhere broke through the defenses of the *status quo*. There was, for example, Lester Frank Ward, a six-foot Illinoisan and onetime Union soldier who worked for years as a government geologist in Washington and filled his leisure time with brisk walking expeditions and the reading of books in many languages. Ward became one of the exponents of the new science of sociology and finally, in 1906, received a chair in the subject at Brown University.

Like Spencer and his followers, Ward accepted the notion that society was an "organism," passing through evolutionary stages of change. These stages could be defined and understood by a detached and dispassionate study of society's institutions (churches, schools, governments, professions) as they related to each other. All such institutions were adaptive mechanisms, designed to function in certain ways, and they could be expanded or discarded, depending on their success in adapting to change. But unlike Spencer or Sumner, Ward refused to admit that mankind itself was helpless to direct such alterations, and he denied that all change was the inevitable result of the struggle for survival. Man, said Ward, had always acted upon his environment, through invention. He had not survived solely through natural causes.

Robert Ingersoll, drawn as the devil's advocate, talks with his client. Ingersoll's impiety grieved American clergymen, but they prayed for his redemption. He commented: "I feel much as the pretty girl did towards the young man who squeezed her hand. 'It pleased him,' she said, 'and it didn't hurt me.'"

In parts of the world locked for three to five months in winter snows, thin-skinned and furless man had reached his highest level of civilization thanks to fire, clothing and houses—all products of "*art*, the wages of thought—fruits of the intellect."

According to Ward, a philosopher who sat by a warm fire on a winter's night and wrote "on paper with pen and ink in the arbitrary characters of a highly developed language" was simply ignoring the real circumstances of his existence if he asserted that civilization was "the result of natural laws, and that man's duty is to let nature alone." Civilization advanced by protecting the weak, increasing the food supply, sheltering the helpless, reducing dependence on the whims of nature. Someday, Ward predicted, man would recognize that nature was passive and man active, that social institutions could be molded in accordance with knowledge about their ability to fill his needs. Then a true "human stage of development" would be reached.

THERE were those in other fields who, like Ward, accepted the idea of man as a creature of environment but claimed that the environment could be both studied and shaped toward chosen ends. (It was generally assumed by all social evolutionists that as man advanced in evolution, his ends would be more ethical.) Ward published his first book, *Dynamic Sociology*, in 1883. Two years before that, a 39-year-old Massachusetts lawyer with a famous name, Oliver Wendell Holmes Jr., had published a series of lectures entitled *The Common Law*. The burden of them was that legal principles were not eternal and reachable by reasoned deduction. Rather, they had changed in response to the changing aspirations of societies over the centuries (and could again do so). Or, in Holmes's own words, "the life of the law has not been logic, it has been experience."

In 1885 a number of young professors of economics met to form the American Economic Association and to issue a statement of its principles. Until then, as one of them remembered, economic study had been confined to the study of "the nature of wealth and the laws which govern its production, exchange and distribution." Richard T. Ely, child of Connecticut Yankees, educated at Columbia and in Germany, and then teaching at Johns Hopkins, objected to this definition. For it singularly ignored the presence of man, who, it would seem, was simply an instrument by which wealth was created, not the end for which it existed. According to classical economics, competition was the magic force that would automatically bring into harmony all the relations that existed among men struggling to make a living. Therefore, any efforts to substitute man-made regulations for competition—or, as Carnegie would have phrased it, "the struggle for survival"—were futile.

Ely and his equally youthful colleagues from Johns Hopkins, Cornell, Columbia and elsewhere would have none of this. They said goodby to *laissez faire*. The principles that their American Economic Association adopted in 1885 boldly announced that the state was "an agency whose positive assistance is one of the indispensable conditions of human progress." Since economics itself was "still in an early stage of its development," the group looked to "historical and statistical study of actual conditions of economic life for the satisfactory accomplishment of that development." They thought that economic transitions could be managed through the medium of a trained bureaucracy such as that emerging before their admiring eyes in Germany.

John Fiske was praised as a historian by philosophers and as a philosopher by historians. Lecturing and writing about evolution, his "orderly mind moved like a stone-crusher" and he converted the boulders of Darwin's concepts into "a flow of gravel that anyone could build a mental road with."

William Graham Sumner, a leading light of American sociology, was a man of "magnificent baldness" in looks and manner. A practical thinker—his motto was "Keep cool and damn metaphysics"—Sumner was once followed down a street by noisy children calling, "Mister, why don't you smile?"

John Dewey, the father of progressive education, rejected the stultifying educational theories of his time. Many philosophers had suggested improvements in teaching methods but seldom put them into practice. Avoiding this "immune monastic respectability," Dewey started schools to spread his ideas.

Oliver Wendell Holmes Jr. was a noted judge for 49 years, 29 of them as the "great dissenter" on the U.S. Supreme Court. While some of his landmark opinions protested infringement of civil liberties, he also warned: "Protection of free speech would not protect a man in falsely shouting fire."

Actual conditions were the subject of scrutiny, and the laws of competition could, presumably, be relegated to histories of economic thought. Yankee humanitarianism and Prussian efficiency might, somehow, be wedded under the approving eye of scientific economics.

Even philosophers, cloistered in their campus studies, were stirred and came out of the misty regions of metaphysics to take a hand. At Harvard, there resided William James, a man first trained in medicine, who then moved to psychology and finally became a highly literate philosopher. It was said of William James that he wrote psychology like a novelist, while his brother Henry wrote novels like a psychologist. William James was arguing as early as the mid-1870s that Spencer was wrong. He did so by pointing out that Spencer's theories did not explain the mysterious processes which produced the countless variations in nature from which the fittest were selected. James preferred to ignore grand schemes of synthetic philosophy which would make all history scientifically foreordained. He wanted rather to see how the individuals who had been selected by the evolutionary process interacted with their immediate environment.

Professor James held that such a study would reveal the fact that the unique individual actually modified his surroundings. "He acts as a ferment," James declared, and changed his surroundings somewhat—just as a new species, in making its appearance, upset the equilibrium among plants and animals in a certain locality. Social evolution was not something in which environment was all and the individual was passive. "The community," said James, "stagnates without the impulse of the individual. The impulse dies away without the sympathy of the community." To his followers, these words demolished the argument for sitting back and permitting the struggle for survival to go on without individual efforts to improve on nature's handiwork.

James was to become famous as the exponent of pragmatism, a philosophical system for concentrating on the discovery of usable truths and ignoring ultimate, abstract problems which could never be solved by anything that could be learned from human experience. In due time another philosopher, John Dewey (born in 1859, the very year of publication of *Origin of Species*), was to come along and overturn the educational world with a variation on pragmatism. Dewey, a stubborn Vermonter who wrote hard, knotty sentences, had a Vermonter's absolute unwillingness to take anything for granted or admit that one man might be better than another.

EVENTUALLY, Dewey came to see the mind itself as an instrument for solving problems presented to man by his surroundings. As soon as it learned enough to cope with the problems which it chose to meet, the mind had in effect altered the problems. New puzzles then arose, and the cycle began again. Mind and knowledge were not stable things; the mind was not a pitcher into which knowledge was poured. They were both constantly interacting with each other; mind (the organism) and knowledge (the environment) were in constant, shifting balance. Thus was evolutionary theory applied to education, though Dewey's influence was not felt until the very end of the century, with the 1899 publication of his *School and Society*, and it remained for later generations to adapt, interpret, misinterpret and debate his teachings.

In medical sciences the fruits of the new, experimental and critical methods of investigation were soon seen in the conquest of epidemics and the spread of the lifesaving discoveries of a Pasteur or a Koch. In physics and chemistry, invention marked the progress of knowledge; the layman who did not understand theoretical electromagnetic studies understood at least that change had overtaken him when he first saw a floodlight or heard a phonograph play. But the impact of the newer studies in economics, sociology and jurisprudence was delayed for a time until a generation of men emerged from the colleges and won election to public office. There they could put the new studies to work in the service of old and new ideals.

B Y the 1890s, then, the Wards, the Jameses, the Holmeses and the Deweys, and many, many others had made their mark. They had fought their battles with the conservative heirs of Darwin, sometimes using the same terminology as their enemies, sometimes inventing new words and concepts, but always insisting that science, rightly understood, left men plenty of room in which to make themselves a new environment. Therefore, there was still need for reform movements. Historians plunged into the comparative study of ancient legal and communal systems, and some professed to see the roots of the town meeting in the ancient tribal rites of the German forest. Political scientists made intensive studies of democratic institutions in modern, centralized nations. Economists applied statistical and historical yardsticks to the question of how a high or low tariff would increase the supply of goods available to a nation or thought about what guideposts of rate making could be set up for a railroad system so as to keep it running with adequate returns to investors and services to customers.

William James, seen in an odd self-portrait, mastered art, medicine, psychology and philosophy. He said he had learned more from his family and travels than from tutors, who viewed their pupils "as so many small slices cut from the loaf of life" on which "to dab the butter of arithmetic and spelling."

Conservatives continued to argue that regulation was the sure road to ruin; and both standpat and reform-minded social Darwinists, looking beyond the boundaries of the United States, also came up with some notions about higher and lower "races" that were to be of considerable consequence in the politics and warfare of the late 19th and 20th Centuries. No issues were settled for good by the turn of the century, but American intellectual life had undergone a revolution.

Almost everyone was still hopeful and agreed with Ward that life in the future would be higher and nobler; they only argued as to whether or not men could, in the here and now, do much about preparing for that future. The confidence that scientific advance could only be benevolent was swellingly expressed in 1895 by an editor of the popular *Century* magazine after he had visited the laboratory of Nikola Tesla, an immigrant inventor who specialized in the phenomena of high-tension electricity. Robert Underwood Johnson spoke for his time when he declared that what he saw there were shapes of

> . . . blessed spirits waiting to be born . . .
> Thoughts, to unlock the fettering chains of Things;
> The Better Time; the Universal Good.
> Their smile is like the joyous break of morn. . . .

Thus, within 40 years after *Origin of Species* was published, evolutionary science had done much to convince Americans that life was more complex than they knew. The forces of growth and economic development had done the same. For most Americans, and particularly for those Americans of the urban middle classes, old-fashioned optimism still was the prevailing note. The dissenters, however, had not yet had their full hearing.

A COMPLEX PROCESS, lithography begins with smoothing a stone. A picture is then drawn on it and "fixed" into the surface. The stone is inked, then it is ready for printing. In stone and on paper, Currier & Ives captured the life and mood of its era.

Time remembered by Currier & Ives

NATHANIEL CURRIER, lithographer, arrived in New York in 1834 and briskly set up shop. Born in Roxbury, Massachusetts, in 1813, apprenticed to his trade in Boston and Philadelphia, Currier thrived on disasters. When a New Orleans hotel collapsed in 1835, Currier quickly brought out a print of the ruins. In 1840 the steamboat *Lexington* blazed and sank in Long Island Sound. Currier's picture of the burning ship, published in an early illustrated newspaper extra, made his small firm famous. In 1852 James Merritt Ives joined the firm as a bookkeeper. Five years later he was a partner in the growing business. Both men liked horses, fires, art and profits. Currier & Ives flourished, publishing some 7,000 prints—more than all of its contemporary competitors combined. From their five-story factory, where artists painted, men printed and women hand-colored pictures, prints went out across the nation and to Europe. Prints were cheap: from five to 25 cents apiece. In America they appeared everywhere—in homes, bars, barber shops, hotels. Documenting their time, with its firemen, farmers, hunters, yachtsmen and dandies, they also mirrored its moods.

The pictures caught the romance and sentiment of the era, its stuffy propriety, its fast-vanishing tang of adventure in the woods and the West. The lithographers composed a panorama extending from the country's young years, when the West was still unwon, the Civil War unfought, up to the century's end. Currier retired in 1880. Ives died in 1895. By then photography and new methods of printing were replacing lithography. But the prints of Currier & Ives remain—a bright, irreplaceable record of 19th Century America.

AN EAGER FIREMAN, Nathaniel Currier is shown in o▮ of his prints. He was a volunteer, as were all Americ▮ firemen until 1853, when Cincinnati formed a paid briga▮

"Preparing for Market" shows a farmer and his wife loading the wagon with produce for the town. Placid rural scenes pleased a public that

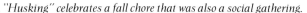

"Husking" celebrates a fall chore that was also a social gathering.

Prints in praise of rural life for crowded city homes

IN 1840, when Nathaniel Currier issued his first best-selling print, less than two million Americans lived in cities. By 1880, when he retired, urban population had grown to more than 14 million. City dwellers, and especially farmers' sons who had left the land, developed a keen nostalgia for country life. At a distance it seemed golden, virtuous and free. Artists enhanced the myth. But rising land values and the need for machines to reap the harvests in the rolling prairies had changed the farmer's life. Farming was a business, and the farmer needed banks and stores, new parts and new machines. The rustic idyl that the artists drew had swiftly passed away.

was increasingly urban. Pressed into cities, thousands adorned their walls with prints that made life in the countryside seem rich and free.

"Getting Ice," once a regular winter chore, is the subject of this rare print of 1864. The ice was stored in sawdust and sold in the summer.

AN EMBATTLED HUNTER fights a hand-to-hand battle with a raging bear. Dramatic scenes such as this were extremely popular. Arthur Fitzwilliam Tait, who painted the original of this picture, did a number of works for Currier & Ives. Fond of the wilds, Tait often left his Broadway studio for his camp in the Adirondacks, where he fished, studied nature and painted.

A WINTER FISHERMAN (*below*) pulls in a trout on Chateaugay Lake in the Adirondacks. Few men were hardy enough to go ice fishing, so the prints provided a vicarious adventure.

A SUMMER MARKSMAN tries for beach snipe. Snipe do not make much of a meal, but their swift, erratic, dipping flight makes them hard targets that only an expert could hope to hit.

The hunt for game and the pursuit of adventure

FOR the frontiersman, hunting and fishing had been a natural and necessary part of life. Moving west ahead of the crowd, he had found unlimited supplies of game. But as the plains were plowed and settled and as the frontier reached the sea, hunting became a personal adventure rather than a search for food. Currier & Ives recorded that adventure in a series of prints on American hunting. These glorified the solitary outdoorsman whose rugged independence, once common in the land, was growing rare. By mid-century the lonely hunter was being replaced by Eastern sportsmen and visiting Englishmen who, finding birds and animals in tremendous abundance, slaughtered game for sport. In one hunt, 41 cougars, 14 wildcats and 111 buffalo were killed. Buffalo Bill Cody boasted that in 17 months he had brought down more than 4,000 buffalo. Currier & Ives, omitting the massacres, romanticized the hunter's saga.

23

A brisk and fancy pastime

Fashionable folks in fancy rigs take a spin through Central Park. In 1856, there were about 20,000 carriages in New York City alone, and the park filled up on Sunday afternoons with couples and dandies out for a ride. For speed, there was the phaeton *(top left)*; for elegant comfort, the landaulet *(top right)*

or the victoria *(bottom center)*. Prices ranged from $350 for a light phaeton to $1,500 for a fancy coach. Colors or coats of arms often distinguished a carriage. The Vanderbilts rode in maroon vehicles, the Astors rode in blue. The Brewsters were the greatest carriage builders of the day. Their workshops pro-duced carriages which, against international competition, won gold medals at the Paris Exhibition of 1878. Abraham Lincoln rode in a Brewster, as did the elite of the East. By the century's end, however, automobiles had begun to appear. In parks and on roads the elegant carriage was slowly replaced by the car.

Racing each other, the New York Yacht Club fleet lines up for a start. Thousands watched from the shore. Printed in 1869, this picture was

A splendor of sail and the thrill of speed

IN 1844 the New York Yacht Club was founded, with John C. Stevens as its first commodore. As a sport, yachting came to maturity fast. In 1851 Commodore Stevens' yacht, the *America*, trounced 14 British boats so badly that an eyewitness sadly reported: "There is no second." With that victory the America's Cup races—won ever since by American boats—began. Among the wealthy, the sport spread. In 1856 the New York *Herald* noted that "yachting—the most expensive, the most healthful, and the most delightful of amusements—has experienced a decided revival." Currier & Ives, as fond of ships as they were of fires, commissioned a large number of pictures that recorded the vessels of their day. Their artists painted clipper ships and iceboats, yachts and packet boats, Chinese junks and steamships. Brighter than words, the prints supplied the nation with a colorful report of life on the seas.

RACING A TRAIN, iceboats on the Hudson take the lead. The boats, as long as 70 feet and with 1,000 square feet of sail, usually won the race. Iceboating was a popular sport of the 1870s.

one of more than 300 marine scenes published by Currier & Ives.

KISS ME QUICK.

Children: this is the third time within an hour that I have placed your hats properly upon your heads.—There!!

Coy humor, gushy sentiment and earnest morality

CURRIER & IVES, "Printmakers to the American People," catered to 19th Century American taste. It was an oddly sentimental taste for a people who had forged a nation and fought a savage Civil War. As if the public had had enough of reality, it turned to an easier world of stalwart virtues, prim courtships and grieving children. Art taught and entertained. *The Drunkard's Progress* showed a drinker's decline from a glass with a friend to death by suicide. *The Ladder of Fortune (right)* assured the virtuous of riches and joy. Favorites in the Currier & Ives catalogue were titles such as *The Lovers Quarrel, Popping the Question, The Sailors Adieu* and thrilling scenes of a mother and child saved from a watery grave by a muscular seaman. On the walls of countless American homes, prints provided people with a setting of melodrama, morality and romance.

HIDING THE INNOCENT EYES of the young, a governess turns to be kissed. "Hugging and kissing," said a manners book, "are all very well when not indulged in too often."

MOURNING A PET, a doleful cortege *(below)* escorts a robin to its grave. Currier & Ives, who advertised "subjects best adapted to suit the popular taste," found a popular taste for tears.

THE STEPS TO SUCCESS attract a small crowd, while sin gains throngs behind. Urban growth alarmed moralists, who agreed that vice inhabited cities and virtue lived down on the farm.

PUBLISHED BY CURRIER & IVES.   Copyright, 1875 by Currier & Ives, N.Y.   125 NASSAU ST. NEW YORK

THE LADDER OF FORTUNE.

Industry and Morality bring solid rewards.   Idle schemes and speculations yield poverty and ruin.

The great Chicago fire

Chicago was dry as tinder in October 1871. For weeks there had been no rain. Most of the city's houses were built of pine. On the night of October 7, a brief blaze roared up, burning four city blocks before it was brought under control. The fire chief was relieved. To protect his city of 300,000, his department

had only 54 hose carts, 15 steam pumpers, and four hook-and-ladder trucks. His men were tired. The next night in the Irish section of Chicago, fire broke out again. It started in a barn, swept up shanties, rose 50 feet and flew northeast, rose higher and leaped the river, blazing its way across the city and out to the lake beyond. For 30 hours the fire raged. Then it began to rain and the fire died out. Two thousand acres had been burned. Two hundred million dollars' worth of property was destroyed, 300 people were dead. Chicago rose from its ashes, but the century's great blaze roars on in a Currier & Ives print.

2. THE WORLD OF THE CITY

"CITIES are the centers of influence," said Dwight L. Moody, the great evangelist, sometime around 1875. "Water runs downhill, and the highest hills in America are the great cities. If we can stir them we shall stir the whole country."

This was a vastly significant insight. The cities had always played an important, if sometimes unhonored role in the American story. But in the early 19th Century, they had somehow faded from the national self-portraiture. The representative American was to be found in a log cabin, in a plantation house, on the deck of a side-wheeler or yoking the oxen to a prairie schooner. No one before 1865 (except, perhaps, Walt Whitman) professed to see him strolling over the cobblestones or reading a newspaper under gaslight. Yet inexorably, and ever more rapidly after the '60s, the city began to suck in a greater share of the people, the wealth, the talent and the attention of the United States of America.

In 1860 four out of five Americans lived in places with less than 2,500 people. In 1900 just about every seventh American lived in a city of more than 250,000 inhabitants. And every 12th American lived in New York, Philadelphia or Chicago. The new cities were everywhere, deriving their powers from some strategic location on the endless stream of traffic from forest, mine or farm to factory and then to market.

New York and San Francisco sat at the gateways to the transoceanic trade

BILANT CHICAGOANS celebrate the part their city
cently become the second largest in the United States)
ayed in electing President Grover Cleveland in 1892.

33

of the Atlantic and Pacific. As early as 1868 a New York booster could declare that "the sea that washes its shores is murmuring of its greatness; the breezes that fan it are whispering of its beauty; the stars that shine over it are silently predicting its excellence." San Francisco's bay was the heart of a big city that rose, proud and gaudy, on steep and wind-blown hills. Poet Joaquin Miller, late in the century, marveled at the harbor's display of "huge ships, black-bellied . . . broad, yellow flags from silken [China], round, blood-red banners from Nippon . . . brave battleships as white as snow, with bannered stars tossed to the wind."

Elsewhere, Pittsburgh and St. Louis sat at the junctions of rivers. Pittsburgh was fast on the way to becoming the nation's great forge. St. Louis, with over 300,000 people by 1870, was hustling valiantly to maintain, by manufacturing, the position it had earned as the gateway to the continent's interior. Now, although some freight boats still plied the Missouri, the highroads to the prairies and mountains were iron ones.

Chicago! As early as 1868 its growth struck a Scottish visitor as "one of the most amazing things in the history of modern civilization." Even then the "gem of the prairie" saw hundreds of lake vessels swarming in and out of its wharves in a year, loaded with millions of bushels of flour and grain, and hundreds of millions of board feet of lumber. Burned to the ground in 1871, Chicago came roaring back to life; passed the million mark in population by 1890; clanged and quivered with the busy sounds of men at work in grain elevators, packing plants, farm machinery factories, freight depots. In 1885, Chicago completed a building rising a full 10 stories above street level. This elevation, breathtaking for its time, was made possible by a new technique which the architect William Jenney had adopted. The floors and masonry walls were supported by a metal framework. Since the masonry bore no weight, it could be built upward to almost any height. Within a few years such architects as Daniel Burnham, John Root and Louis Sullivan had made Chicago the birthplace of the skyscraper. Long before the 20th Century began, Chicago was, in Carl Sandburg's words, "Hog Butcher, Tool Maker, Stacker of Wheat, Player with Railroads and Freight Handler to the Nation."

And there were the other cities of prairie, gulf, bay and river. Mark Twain, on a reminiscent tour of the Mississippi in 1882, noted that New Orleans was "a driving place commercially," its streets already beginning to twinkle with electric lights. At the other end of the Mississippi, St. Paul and Minneapolis struck him as full of "newness, briskness, swift progress, wealth, intelligence . . . and general slash and go and energy."

Philadelphia, with "interminable rows of clean-shaven warehouses and shops," Richmond and Atlanta covering the scars of war with new buildings, Cleveland and Cincinnati and Omaha and Memphis and Denver, cities all over the land were exercising their economic magnetism on the back country.

THERE were new technological problems to be solved, as hundreds of thousands of men and women had to be housed, moved from shop to home and provided with food by the freight-car and barge load, with mountains of fuel and water by the millions of gallons. Invention began to change the face of the cities, as the cities themselves changed the face of the nation. New York was, as always, a pacemaker if not always an originator in such changes. In 1870, it inaugurated an elevated railway that ran for several miles along

Charles Brush's electric lighting (above) first brightened Broadway in 1880; 21 months later Edison's incandescent lamps helped light up downtown Manhattan. These new lights, burning all night, started such a craze for the new lighting that by 1900 electrified offices, hotels and theater marquees had literally turned old Broadway into the "Great White Way."

Ninth Avenue. Steam locomotives raced overhead, raining sparks and cinders on a proud but apprehensive public. Soon the "El" was to be seen on Second, Third and Sixth Avenues as well. In 1877 the first telephone was installed in the city. In 1880 C.F. Brush's arc lights were the first electric street lights to be operated commercially in New York.

On May 24, 1883, a 14-year epic came to an end with the opening of the Brooklyn Bridge, spanning the East River from Manhattan to the still-independent city of Brooklyn. It was the longest suspension bridge in the world. Yet Brooklyn Bridge was not big enough to accommodate the streams of humanity across the river to and from Manhattan daily. In 1889 the Washington Bridge across the Harlem River sped travel to the Bronx. Work began in 1896 on a second East River span. Meanwhile, between 1885 and 1892, engineers had driven new tunnels to the Croton watershed. The enlarged aqueducts had a capacity of nearly 300 million gallons a day, but within 20 years New York was digging its way up to the Catskills for more water.

As the 20th Century began, the tunnel for the city's first successful subway (the Interborough Rapid Transit) was being dug and the elevated lines were being electrified. The Flatiron Building, 20 stories tall, was only two years away from completion and the transient glory of being New York's most famous skyscraper. On a more somber note, 1900 also was the year in which a New York State Tenement House Commission found that on Manhattan alone, where more than a million people lived in some 43,000 crowded tenement houses, "adequate light and air, perfect sanitation, even passable home environment" could not be provided by the best house of this kind. The slum was as much a part of the 20th Century New York scene as the skyscraper.

ELSEWHERE, other cities took on a form familiar to modern eyes. Thirty million square yards of asphalt paving were poured onto American streets by 1898, and the rattle of wheels on cobblestones, where they still existed, was a vanishing sound, touched with the quaintness of a "period" restoration.

In 1873 cable cars first gave San Franciscans a dizzying ride to and from their chosen places of work and amusement. In 1888 the first successful commercially operated stretch of electric railway over city streets was opened in Richmond. Seven years later, there were 10,000 miles of such electric urban transit lines in the country. By 1878 there were public waterworks in 600 American cities, a number multiplied almost six times in the next 20 years. Provision for sewers and garbage disposal began to appear, or to bulk larger, in municipal budgets. City-controlled water supplies reduced the incidence of typhoid and put an end to the cholera epidemics which had swept even advanced cities like New York from time to time. But tuberculosis was prevalent in the airless and densely packed tenements of the poorer city districts. This was sobering evidence of urban poverty, one of the most serious problems of metropolitan life.

The underlying changes brought by large-scale urbanism were in modern styles of life and thought to be found everywhere, molding new patterns and figures out of old clay. The very names carried by these innovations—yellow journalism, the new woman, the boss, the vice district—tell something of their strangeness and suggest a little of their impact.

The newspaper and the town were partners from the time that the first single-page journal appeared in Boston in 1690. After the Civil War, the

A San Francisco cable car makes its steep uphill run along Clay Street. One of the inventions that changed the face of growing cities, the cable car was installed in 1873 by Andrew Hallidie, a wire-rope manufacturer. He had to conduct the first downhill run himself when the driver, or "gripman," stared down the plunging slope into lower San Francisco and then blanched.

alliance flourished, helped by invention and expansion. Beginning in the '60s, the development of improved printing methods, of a usable typesetting machine and of wood-pulp paper made possible the daily miracle of producing many thousands (ultimately hundreds of thousands) of copies of newspapers.

Armed with these technological marvels, the successful editor was one who provided his readers with sensational exploits: news flashed across transoceanic cables, "inside" interviews, lurid tales of sin and slaughter in places high and low, eyewitness reports of battles fought in such faraway places as Plevna, in Bulgaria. The newspaper did more than bring the world to the doorstep every morning. Across its pages were spread advertisements extolling the products of industrial America, from baby food to sewing machines. Publishers soon discovered that lucrative advertising increased with circulation, and that larger circulation could be achieved by a variety of offerings, some new in the 1870s and 1880s, some introduced 30 or 40 years before. Among the older features were serialized novels, sporting news and police-court reports, as well as the commercial, financial and political news. There were also such heralds of a new day in journalism as banner headlines, fashion notes and funny cartoons in color. These last appeared in the '90s, when the Sunday editions of the New York *World* displayed no fewer than eight pages of primitive "funnies," four in color. One such cartoon was entitled "Hogan's Alley," featuring the rowdy antics of a number of urchins, one of them dressed in a violent yellow garment imperfectly resembling a nightshirt. "The Yellow Kid" became so popular that when a dignified critic was once groping for a label to apply to lowbrow popular journalism, he remembered "The Kid" and aimed a brickbat at "the yellow press."

So a name was born. Yellow journalism, with its emphasis on the blaring headline, the juicy ax-murder (with drawings and, by 1900, photographs) and the high-society divorce, was not quite synonymous with big-time newspaper publication. There were papers like the Kansas City *Star* which became extraordinarily successful without sensationalism. They built big circulations by lively reporting and editorializing, by taking out after boodlers and malefactors in their hometowns, and by furnishing an abundance of entertainment and advertisement for a daily price that generally stayed at two cents—cheaper by subscription. As the versifier Eugene Field noted of the Kansas City paper: "Twinkle, twinkle, little Star— / Bright and gossipy you are; / We can daily hear you speak / For a paltry dime a week."

T HE father of the yellow press was Joseph Pulitzer, a man whose life was woven of sparkling success and dark strands of personal anguish. Born in Hungary, he arrived in Boston in 1864, an undernourished teen-age recruit for the Union army. A few years later, he was a reporter for a German-language newspaper in St. Louis, angularly legging it to stories with his coattails flying. In 1878 he had done well enough to buy two St. Louis papers, the *Post* and the *Dispatch*, which he combined into a great and enduring journal.

In 1883 Pulitzer plunged into New York City journalism with the purchase of a more or less down-at-the-heels paper, the New York *World*. Into it he poured unlimited imagination and energy. To it he brought an instinct for the popular taste and a consistently correct judgment of the temper of the times. The *World*'s editorials lashed bossism, trusts, the high tariff, oppressive employers. Its crusades ran from denouncing the Bell telephone monopo-

Finding Doctor Livingstone in Africa, Henry Stanley of the New York "Herald" ends his arduous search. To locate the missing British missionary, the "Herald" laid out over $40,000. "I make news," boasted the paper's owner, James G. Bennett. In its mad scramble for scoops, the "Herald" published the news of Custer's Last Stand four days ahead of its competitors.

ly to collecting $100,000, much of it in nickels and dimes, to build the pedestal for the Statue of Liberty. The *World's* reporters doubled as actors. They pretended to be working girls, immigrants, lunatics and lobbyists in order to get inside stories, all blazoned on the front page.

The *World's* feature writers and artists sketched socialites and pugilists, prime ministers and matinee idols—treating them all impartially by the single standard of whether they made bright copy. The *World's* circulation staff used every trick they could think of to increase readership—among them picnics, excursions and charity-basket giveaways. As a result of this feverish ingenuity, the *World* was selling 250,000 copies daily by 1887.

Pulitzer himself was a sick man—his eyes were lapsing into total blindness, his lungs wheezed and his nerves screamed at noise. By 1890 he was forced into absentee ownership, directing his papers from a yacht or seaside resorts, through telegrams and memoranda. Five years later he met his match when William Randolph Hearst came into New York to buy the New York *Journal.* Hearst had his father's mining millions to support his contest with the *World,* and he hired away star staffmen from the *World,* outdid Pulitzer in sensations and forced the older man to follow suit.

IN New York and elsewhere the mammoth newspapers gave the cities something they needed. They furnished a polyglot, swarming population with a sense of civic identity as they trumpeted "Chicago's demands" or "New York's welcome to her heroes." They gave mixed classes and nationalities a common daily experience of reading.

The urbanite had other places to which he could turn for recreation. The well-educated might read the "better" magazines—*The Century, Lippincott's, Harper's, The Atlantic, Scribner's.* The standard fare of these monthlies included serialized novels or short stories by well-known writers like William Dean Howells, Mark Twain, George Washington Cable, Joel Chandler Harris, Sarah Orne Jewett and Bret Harte. Increasingly, there appeared engravings and drawings, reminiscences of Civil War days and poetry that either struggled to be funny through dialect, or to be uplifting and artistic.

In a large place like New York or Chicago, there was the theater, where good actors such as John Drew (uncle of the Barrymore clan) or Edwin Booth (always haunted by his brother's assassination of Lincoln) or Joseph Jefferson played in revivals of Shakespeare and Restoration writers—or in contemporary dramas now mercifully forgotten.

The city dweller with other tastes might read an illustrated periodical like the *Police Gazette* (founded in New York in 1845). The *Gazette* featured plenty of pictures of scantily clad girls in long black stockings, and it also had a good deal of news of the semi-illegal world of bare-knuckled pugilism. Although generally forbidden by law, prize fighting depended on a city audience. It was in New Orleans in 1892 that the Boston Strong Boy, John L. Sullivan, lost his heavyweight championship to Gentleman Jim Corbett.

Professionalized amusement also cut across social lines, and it was not undignified even for a clergyman to watch an "exhibition" of professional "Base Ball," as the papers of the day spelled it. Starting as an amateur craze, played in open fields by clubs of gentlemen before the Civil War, the game had gradually been taken over by full-time performers and transferred to enclosed grounds. In 1876, the eight-team National League was born and in 1882 it was

Readers gasped while Nellie Bly (Elizabeth Cochrane's pen name), with gripsack and traveling cap, sped around the world in 72 days, wiring dispatches back to the New York "World." In France she met Jules Verne, whose "Tour of the World in 80 Days" had inspired the feat. For a story Nellie would do anything—she once had herself committed to an insane asylum!

challenged by the American Association for the revenues of big-town ball. During the '80s the leagues were dominated by the Chicago White Stockings and the St. Louis Browns. The same decade saw the initiation of a postseason series between the two league winners (temporarily dropped in the '90s), the catcher's mitt, the hit-and-run play and other elements that still are a part of the annual summer-long ritual.

It did not matter whether the city dweller was screaming enthusiasm for a well-placed bunt or listening to Booth rage magnificently through *Richard III*. Whether he was a devotee of sport or the theater, he was in addition a passive participant in an entertainment venture on a commercial scale. The world of the townsman had new scenes and new sounds; the roar of the crowd was one of them. No matter if his taste was high or low, vaudeville or grand opera, the metropolitan idler had a pleasant sense that life offered him a richer diet, a more kaleidoscopic perspective, than it did to his country cousin. Confinement, noise and a lack of fresh air did not seem, to many, too steep a price for such advantages. As for women, if the pitfalls of the city were more numerous, the prospects were more attractive.

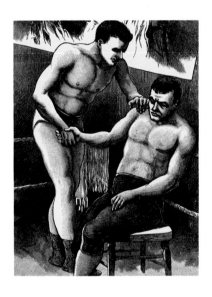

The pink-paged "Police Gazette" gave its readers racy woodcuts, Broadway gossip and backstairs scandal. In order to promote its gaudy sports page, the "Gazette" spent a decade looking for challengers to box champion John L. Sullivan, until Gentleman Jim Corbett (below) defeated him in 1892.

FOR a woman, leaving the farm was a flight from unendurable dependent drudgery. The city, even the factory, promised release from a life dominated by muscle and mulepower, from household chores of staggering proportions, from the loneliness imposed by isolation. Country girls had begun to stream into the New England cotton mills early in the 19th Century. In the booming post-Civil War era, women took their place wherever invention was likely to turn a particular manufacturing process into a matter of pressing treadles or adjusting levers. Women machine-stitched boots and bonnets, pasted labels, assembled and painted small items, and moved noiselessly into other jobs in lofts, shops and warehouses.

The motives behind hiring women workers were far from humanitarian. Employers took advantage of custom to skimp on women's pay, and many a girl who came off a train from the hinterlands, or from an immigrant ship found that she had entered a pinched and drudging life in an unsanitary sweatshop that was often a firetrap.

A cut above the girl who worked in the factory stood the young woman whose voice and manners were good enough to qualify her for certain other jobs. She might be a salesgirl in a mammoth department store. Quite soon after the acceptance by business of the typewriter, it was surrendered to the ladies. The telephone exchanges, too, were not long in putting women at the switchboards. (The legend was that men had first been used, but showed a tendency to explode into profanity, over open lines, when the primitive telephone equipment acted up.) In all phases of what would be called white-collar work, in fact, the utility of woman, with her "sedentary habits, patience, quickness, neatness and gentle manners," was obvious.

Moving up the social scale, when the public school began to flourish a new world was opened to the girl who craved independence. In the year 1890-1891, the number of pupils in all precollegiate schools swelled to approximately 69 of every 100 youngsters between the ages of five and 17. This meant that there were then about 13 million pupils enrolled in public schools. The capacity of women for imparting education was too evident to be missed.

In 1889-1890, at the outset of Benjamin Harrison's Administration, there were approximately 238,000 women teachers at work in the public schools compared to 125,500 men. In some places, like Massachusetts, the ratio of women to men ran as high as 9 to 1. If a young lady lifted her gaze to other professional pinnacles, there were even a few shining examples of women doctors and lawyers. Mrs. Belva Lockwood, admittedly above average, was the first woman lawyer to be admitted to practice before the Supreme Court of the United States.

It was no wonder that the growing number of upper-middle-class girls who could afford to do so were knocking at the gates of the colleges—both the co-educational state institutions and the women's schools like Vassar (opened in 1865), Wellesley (1875), Smith (1875) and Bryn Mawr (1885). Once enrolled, these girls insisted on being prepared in every department of study open to men. As one miss tartly wrote, when counseled against the unfeminine pursuit of higher mathematics: "I will avoid equations, / And shun the naughty surd, / I must beware the perfect square, / Through it young girls have erred: / And when men mention Rule of Three / Pretend I have not heard."

By 1890 American cities were becoming accustomed to the presence of the working woman. She might be in domestic service, or pounding a typewriter, or tending a machine; she might be teaching eight-year-olds to spell, or writing "sob sister" material for Pulitzer or delivering babies; wherever she was, she was there to stay—in numbers amounting at that date to some four million. Yet the story of the new woman did not quite end there.

In 1874, for example, bands of women appeared on the streets of cities like Cincinnati and Pittsburgh to do battle with the liquor evil. The temperance movement had been in existence for years. Now the pressure was increased as clusters of ladies knelt in the mud outside the swinging doors, or even on the sawdust-covered floor of the saloon itself, and prayed loudly for God to bring drunkards to the light. Sheepish pleas and even threats from the owner only raised the volume of the hymns and invocations, and since even a fairly calloused drinker found himself uncomfortable in such unlikely surroundings, a number of barrooms were prayed out of business.

In that year of 1874, the Woman's Christian Temperance Union, composed of ardent female crusaders, was formed. Soon the W.C.T.U. would become a formidable power in the land. Women were also forming themselves into other clubs, which mingled social companionship, uplift and reform in proportions that were intermittently agreeable. Some 400 such groups joined to create a General Federation of Women's Clubs in 1889.

THAT same year, a frail young daughter of the Midwest named Jane Addams turned herself into a symbol of a new kind of woman's work. To the minds of most Americans, her name came to be synonymous with the term "social worker." She leased a residence called Hull-House in a multilingual and dirt-poor section of Chicago. In the years that followed, helped by friends and associates, she devoted herself to making Hull-House a beacon of education, hope and concern to the forgotten urban poor. "Settlement-house" was the name given to such a neighborhood center, with its day nurseries, gymnasiums and classes in language and other subjects for slum dwellers. As additional settlement houses were founded during the '90s, in other large cities, they too offered new outlets for the energies of women.

By the end of the century, there was indication of a change in the status of

"The Ladies Home Journal" was founded in 1883 as part of a farm paper and soon covered everything from homemaking tips to political news and plans for cheap homes.

The comic paper "Puck," begun in German, quickly became an American staple. To its bold political cartoons were added wry ballads, comments and barbed epigrams.

The "Century" gave genteel readers of the 1880s illustrated fictional memoirs of the ante-bellum South written in quaint old slave dialect. It also ran the Uncle Remus tales.

"Life," begun in 1883 as a literate, satiric weekly, prospered for decades until others entered the growing field. Then in 1936 the "Life" title was purchased by Time Inc.

women in the mounting statistics of female employment. In the new America, and particularly in the cities, where more opportunities were available, women were emerging from the cocoon.

The growth of the city had its effect on politics, too. Bosses flourished in the state capitals and in Washington itself, but the big-city boss ran a tougher empire and was apt to have more picturesque gifts. In order to win popularity with lower-class urban voters, it was necessary to be one of them. More often than not, the city boss had grown up in the "rat-infested rookeries" of the workingmen's districts, where "souls and bodies were saved by the parish priest, the family doctor, and the local political saloonkeeper . . . who knew everyone and was the link between the exploited immigrant and the incomprehensible, distant law."

In such a steamy urban jungle, a young man handy with his fists and tongue was likely to win friends who would show their affection in the form of a vote-as-requested on election day. This gave the future leader a negotiable commodity to take to party headquarters. From there on, it was up to him. New recruits for his ranks could be won by gifts of food and drink, judiciously distributed cash and, ultimately, jobs in the city government's numerous departments. Enough ward and district leaders, combined in a "ring," could eventually control the election of aldermen and judges, and run the city according to their tastes, which were apt to be expensive.

Exposing the varieties of vice kept many a reporter and artist busy as city life quickened in the late 1800s. Scandal was grist for the mills of such publications as the "Police Gazette." Each month, there were new "crimes of the clergy" (above) or police raids on a "house of ill repute" (below). Slums, vice, graft and crime were part and parcel of the urbanized America.

Some of the money to keep the process functioning came from petty graft—the protection money slipped to the policeman on the beat by the bartender and dutifully passed on (with deductions en route) to the commissioner and, ultimately, the reigning boss of the locality. But the really big takings were made possible by the fact that the enormous work of modernizing the cities involved millions of dollars.

The corporation which wanted a streetcar franchise or a permit to build a power station had to get the approval of a common council or a board of aldermen. Individual members of these bodies were apt to be demanding and undisciplined. The boss served as a useful coordinator of corporate needs and governmental demands. As Tammany's Richard Croker put it to a young New York reporter one day in the 1890s: ". . . There's a mayor *and* a council *and* judges *and*—a hundred other men to deal with. A government is nothing but a business, and you can't do business with a lot of officials, who check and cross one another and who come and go, there this year, out the next. A business man wants to do business with one man. . . ."

Bosses came in assorted shapes and sizes. One of the best known in the 19th Century was William M. Tweed of New York, probably because his downfall, in 1871, was the result of a spectacular assault by the press. Tweed represented a swaggering vulgarity which was not always typical of the bosses. That pragmatic philosopher of organization politics, Richard Croker, was Tammany's chieftain from 1886 to 1901. Croker was a prudent and unostentatious businessman who dealt in votes wholesale and lived like other executives. He perfected the art of "honest graft"—such as getting a friend's insurance firm all sorts of city business. He also brought order and organization to the routine of shakedowns by city employees and let subordinates attend to the petty graft and the ballot-box stuffing and vote repeating. When reformers raised a hue and cry, he retired to Ireland and raised blooded horses.

James McManes, the Republican boss of Philadelphia in the 1870s, was a thrifty and taciturn investor in real estate, street railways and banks. As one of the trustees of Philadelphia's municipal gas system, he had used his patronage power to build up a core of faithful workers who eventually gave him party control. Though McManes looked respectable, his cost was as high as that of more raffish bosses. Philadelphia's debt shot up $50 million between 1860 and 1881, when the Gas Ring was in power, though it remained "badly paved, badly cleansed, badly supplied with gas [and] water."

The boss and his lieutenants were a trial to righteousness. Not only were they expensive, but they smelled of the back alleys that were part of their domain. When two of Chicago's aldermen, "Hinky-Dink" Kenna and "Bathhouse John" Coughlin, wanted "contributions," they got them by selling their supporters tickets to a huge annual ball. The ordinarily invisible rank and file of the organization would then emerge into the light for the world to see— "pickpockets . . . scarlet women and the yellow men who live from and by them; bartenders; professional repeaters . . . saloon bouncers; prizefight promoters; liquor salesmen; police captains; runners for gambling houses. . . ."

"Yellow Journalists" Pulitzer and Hearst are washed over the falls of public protest in the bucket of their "New Journalism" in this 1897 cartoon. As their papers outdid each other in sensationalism, the "Journal" and "World" were barred from such places as public libraries, YMCAs and the Princeton Theological Seminary. Still, sales rose faster than the protests.

THE "good people" looked, held their noses and blamed municipal corruption on the dregs of society. The immigrants were the particular targets of upper-crust wrath. For the ward heelers and precinct captains—those administrators of a primitive tit-for-tat welfare program—could generally count on getting the votes of the newcomers. In return for his ballot, the bewildered immigrant could expect the help of the leader, and his mysterious powers of "fix," in an unintelligible world of new rules and laws. But the reformers who periodically rose up and set back a machine for a year or two overlooked more fundamental causes of machine government.

One was the withdrawal of the "best people" themselves into the world of business. As Rudyard Kipling noticed, during a visit to San Francisco in 1889, an American "has not time to vote for turn-cocks and district attorneys and cattle of that kind. . . ." Since the right kind of people would not concern themselves with politics, they left the field wide open to others who would, and did. The length and complexity of the urban ballot, with its innumerable elected judges, assessors and commissioners—a relic of the Jacksonian era's passion for popular choice of officeholders—also made it easy for the machine which selected the aspirants for office to dominate a city's administration without much challenge. Who knew—or knows today—the qualifications of the candidates for probate judge or waterworks supervisor?

The reformers also overlooked, in their complaints, the alliance between boodling politicians and the proprietors of big business. Those who decried machine politics did not always ask themselves exactly *how* the corporations in which they held stock received franchises or tax rebates or injunctions against competitors and strikers.

Above all, reformers were only spasmodically interested in government— usually their activity was limited to the few months before an election, while it was the boss's full-time job. And the reformers had a blind spot brilliantly spotlighted by "Mr. Dooley," a fictional Irish Catholic bartender-philosopher created in the '90s by a Chicago newspaper columnist, Finley P. Dunne. The boss knew, as the comfortable, Anglo-Saxon Protestant uplifter did not, that "there's a few hundherds iv thousands iv people livin' in a part iv th' town that looks like nawthin' but smoke fr'm th' roof iv th' Onion League Club that have on'y two pleasures in life, to wur-ruk an' to vote, both iv which they do at th' uniform rate iv wan dollar an' a half a day."

The boss was a product of urban bigness. He produced, crookedly and expensively, but with effect, a new style of political cohesion and organization to meet the vastly expanded needs of the city. Honest politics was eventually going to have to learn to meet those needs, in the process jettisoning many outmoded ideas of the superiority of Jeffersonian, hands-off, rigidly limited and economical government. Jefferson had neither liked nor understood cities. Around 1900, the nation which justly did him honor was beginning to find out that it could not afford to share his prejudices.

JEFFERSON'S suspicions of the cities ignored their tremendous creative potential. They united leisure, opulence, challenges and talent in a way that produced civilization, as his reading of ancient and Renaissance history should have taught Thomas Jefferson, had he not been so much in love with the life of a Virginia planter. Nonetheless the doubts of the Sage of Monticello might have seemed confirmed by the slums and nurseries of crime which disfigured almost all the major towns of the late 19th Century United States.

New York had its Tenderloin and its Five Points; Chicago its Sands; San Francisco its Barbary Coast; other towns, their own places where it was unsafe to walk at night, where honky-tonks ran at full blast around the clock, and where murder, theft, prostitution and drug peddling were the commonplaces of existence. Periodically, right-minded ministers, followed by a gaggle of reporters, would descend into these neighborhoods, look their fill at the peep shows, stiffly permit themselves to be approached by the harlots, and then emerge to demand a cleanup. And, periodically, the police would round up a few dozen exemplars of the life of sin, fire a few sacrificial bribetakers and—temporarily—call off vice operations.

Close by the vice districts, and furnishing them with fresh prospects every year, were the slums. As city populations shot upward, real-estate owners found the temptation irresistible to pack poverty-stricken newcomers into tenements as densely as possible. From the safe vantage point of a suburban residence, landlords could count their profits without the distraction of personal observation of the misery they had fostered. In 1890 New York, at least, learned what its underside looked like when an angry young Danish immigrant reporter, Jacob Riis, published his *How the Other Half Lives*.

Riis's book was beset by some of the common errors of its time—notably the notion that certain nationality groups were particularly vulnerable to dirt, alcoholism and greed. But it was also compassionate and tough. It is still strong medicine for weak stomachs. Riis described four- and five-story buildings in which 16 or 20 families, totaling 100 or more people, lived, each family jammed into three tiny rooms which occupied one quarter of a floor. He painted a graphic picture of dimly lit, airshaft-ventilated closets, which served as bedrooms for three and four children; of rickety stairways choked with refuse; of stopped-up common privies.

No one could read the book without smelling the staleness and hopelessness of the tenement or understanding the dreadful mortality in them (particularly among infants), and shuddering at the fires which periodically roared through decaying blocks of slum apartment houses. No one with much per-

"Prohibition is coming!" warns an 1886 cartoon from "Puck." While women crusaded against drinking, and temperance was taught even in Sunday schools, many sober citizens scoffed at prohibition. It was said that for each saloon closed two more sprang up in its place. Other "reform movements" of the time, such as woman's suffrage, were equally scorned by the public.

ception could fail to appreciate why workingmen who spent up to half their income to rent such dens felt hopelessly trapped, or why some children graduated easily to crime and vice.

Such were—such are—the urban slums. They were not easy for a nation to get used to. In the rural world the gap between rich and poor had not been so great, or so shocking. Some wealthy Americans, who could afford to do so, headed back for the country, as improved train service and the development of sewers, roads, water mains and gasworks around the edges of the cities made suburban life possible. By the '90s, a magazine was already speaking of "Harlem, Brooklyn, the Oranges [and] Yonkers" as "dormitories of New York."

Other cities were facing the same exodus, and still do. As the well-off fled, they took their tax revenues, their churches and their concern with urban problems with them. Even before the coming of the auto, which stepped up the tempo, the slums were abandoned, as it were, both by God (or at least by His more respectable parishioners) and man. These depressed areas were gingerly reoccupied by the settlement-house worker, exposed by the crusading reporter, exploited by the criminal and utilized by the politician. That some hardy souls managed to escape the blighting effects of such surroundings into useful lives was a tribute to the stubbornness of the human will for bringing good out of evil, as well as the reverse. They constituted a political and social problem which government would hesitantly begin to approach just as the century was ending.

THE vice district and the slum were prize exhibits for those defenders of the yeoman virtues who insisted that the farm was the only place for republican purity to survive. According to one bit of doggerel: "The city has many attractions, / But think of the vices and sins, / When once in the vortex of fashion, / How soon the course downward begins." The lure and magnetism of metropolis could not be resisted. There was a sense of insecurity behind the outraged cries of small town and rural spokesmen who denounced the city as the home of alien faiths, political rot and triumphant evil. The countryside was losing out. The landholder was foundering in a sea of economic problems. He was also forfeiting his social pre-eminence and this lent a fresh urgency to his complaints. The city might be Babylon, but it was a Babylon made for a people on the hustle. As Franklin Wilson, a commentator of the Grant era, put it with finality:

> For the Mechanical, Commercial, and Professional classes a location in or near *a city* is unquestionably the best. Where one would act directly on men, deal with men, or employ much human labor, he ought to be where men are densely congregated. . . . That is to be preferred which is . . . most advantageously situated by its proximity to the mines or quarries, the cotton or grain fields, its ample manufacturing and commercial facilities for making, receiving, and distributing goods of all kinds; most distinguished for the probity and moral worth of its citizens, and its institutions for promoting education, science, art, religion, and benevolence. Such a city cannot fail to be a growing one, and a grand field for honorable enterprise.

To which a dozen cities with their universities, museums and libraries—as well as their saloons and bordellos—might have nodded in confident agreement. Babylon held the trump cards in its offices and factories, and Babylon was going to win.

Flouting convention, Dr. Mary Walker wore pants, frock coat and high silk hat to President Chester Arthur's 1882 New Year's reception. Besides practicing medicine, she served as an officer in the Civil War. The public was scandalized by her attire. Boys threw rotten eggs, women made faces at her in the street and one humorist labeled her a "self-made man."

Two Gibson girls turn the head of a man about town. Gibson's drawings set a style for the gay decade.

The gay nineties: society at play

By 1890 the chores of expansion and the exhaustion of civil war were over. Railways knit the continent; and now the wealth dug out of it could be lavishly spent. "Hell, I'm rich!" roared Diamond Jim Brady, Lillian Russell's constant friend. "It's time I had some fun!" He spoke not only for himself but for all who could afford to play. Certainly "The 400"—the magnificent few who could fit into Mrs. Astor's ballroom—had the money, and so did the shapely ladies *(above)* drawn by Charles Dana Gibson. Gibson portrayed the fashionable world busy at its new amusements. In 1890 the second Madison Square Garden opened; the bicycle fad was beginning; vaudeville and melodrama enjoyed their heyday. It was a time when, Clarence Day wrote, "we liked flesh. It didn't have to be bare, and it wasn't, but it had to be there." Lillian Russell *(right)* added a fine soprano voice to a fair amount of flesh and was the darling of the decade. As lavish as the age, she put away a 13-course dinner with ease and rode a bicycle that glittered with diamonds. Flesh appeared on the beaches too. American dress, and American women, became more free. Faced with this threat, men retreated to plush clubs and bars. It was also a time of travel for the rich: on yachts, or overseas to buy an English manor house. Parties were popular; daughters were married off to foreign lords, false or real. But the gaiety of the '90s was the gaiety of wealth. It scarcely touched more than half of New York's population, who lived in tenements, or the annual flood of impoverished immigrants. As the nation moved into the 20th Century, trolleys and cars replaced the bicycle, movies took over the stage and, as wealth spread, the glitter of an exclusive society dimmed.

LUSCIOUS STAGE STAR, Lillian Russell is heftier than th Gibson girl. A famous singer, fond of diamonds, men an cycling, she lived with a gusto that was typical of the time

The Bradley Martin ball of 1897 brings society out in dress and gems worth hundreds of thousands of dollars. So extravagant was the ball

A would-be aristocracy in a prosperous democracy

Gibson-girl daughters teach Father how to spend money abroad.

IN 1890 the satirical magazine *Life* noted that "The 400" had grown to 1,500. Wall Street, *Life* explained, had got control and watered the stock. The newly rich jostled for position. Mr. Randolph Guggenheim threw a party at the Waldorf at which hired nightingales sang from transplanted rose trees. Liqueurs bottled before the French Revolution were served. At the Bradley Martin ball, one man appeared in golden armor valued at $10,-000; other courtly democrats tripped over their swords as they danced. Teddy Roosevelt, New York's police commissioner, was invited to the ball, but he replied: "My wife's going because she's got her costume. . . . I shall be outside looking after the police." Such rude humor offended Ward McAllister, "the Autocrat of Drawing-Rooms," who struggled to construct a modern monarchy with Mrs. William Astor as its social queen. Faced with mocking criticism, society went yachting, built summer homes in Newport—like Marble House, Mrs. W. K. Vanderbilt's $11 million birthday present from her husband—or left for Europe, where royalty still mattered.

at the Waldorf that the Martins' tax assessment was doubled. The family moved abroad.

SUPREME SNOB Ward McAllister's phrase "The 400" indicates his efforts to maintain an elite society.

EXTREME NEED and extreme riches meet on a pier. While New York Yacht Club members chatted, paupers and criminals were being sent off to the city's island institutions.

AN ORNATE TOWER marking Madison Square Garden (*left*) rises 341 feet. Designed by Stanford White, opened in 1890, the Garden housed the socially important National Horse Show.

A FANCY PRIZE is awarded by the ringmaster as officials look on. English experts were often imported to judge the horse shows, which were the first event in society's winter season.

New York's sumptuous palace for the horsy set

MADISON SQUARE GARDEN was the show place of New York in the '90s. Housing the city's circuses, bicycle displays and six-day races, it also held the year's pre-eminent sporting and social event, the National Horse Show. In 1891 the show received $35,000 from the sale of boxes. Society came to be seen. One *Life* joke ran: "Are you exhibiting in the Horse Show this year?" "Yes, I'm sending my daughter." The beautiful roof garden drew crowds, and Saint-Gaudens' statue of Diana, atop the tower, drew outraged criticism from moralists, for Diana was America's first nude female statue on permanent public display. The Garden's architect, Stanford White, had an apartment in the tower where he threw parties wild even for the time. At one, a naked lady reportedly stepped out of an enormous cake to serve dessert; 11 others came to help her. In 1900 the first National Automobile Show was held at the Garden. By 1905 society's attendance at the Horse Show was dwindling. It had become, some felt, too common.

At the Horse Show, men look at Gibson women, women at each other. Boxes cost more than $400.

49

A bishop goes for a healthy excursion with pretty Gibson girls.

A model in sporting attire shows women how to manage a bicycle.

The spectacular craze that swept the country

BICYCLING, "the most spectacular craze of all," was taking hold in 1890. Before, an eccentric few had ridden their awkward "machines." The pneumatic tire and improved design made the sport possible for all. By 1893 a million Americans were cycling; soon after, a million bicycles were being manufactured yearly. Stage stars took to the sport *(below)* to keep their figures trim and their names in the news. Diamond Jim

LILLIAN RUSSELL sits on a Two-Speed Changeable-Geared Racycle. The singer's second bike, glittering with gold, was kept in a leather case. She rode through Central Park daily.

EUGENE SANDOW, "The Monarch of Muscle," bulges aboard his bike. Sandow, who could lift a piano with an eight-man band playing on top, found "a spin" on his wheel fine exercise.

From left to right, she illustrates methods of "carrying the bicycle, walking it, mounting from peg, dismounting, wheeling and coasting."

Brady gave Lillian Russell a gold-plated, jewel-studded bicycle and kept a dozen gilded ones for himself. The average bicycle, however, cost between $100 and $125. Bicycle parades and races were organized. Even society acknowledged the craze and formed the Michaux Club, named after a pioneer bicycle dealer. Members, including Vanderbilts, drilled in armories to band music.

For women the sport was emancipating. More simple fashions were introduced and women became at home out of doors. Sunday was the great day for the sport. While some preachers lamented the fact, insisting "you cannot serve God and skylark on a bicycle," other people bravely mounted and rode. In 1900 the fad ended as suddenly as it began. In the cities commuting trains and trolleys replaced the bicycle. Only the effects remained: raised hems, more sensible clothes and freer women.

ANNA HELD, a popular singer, poses raptly beside her two-wheeler. Anna came from London in 1896 at the peak of the bicycle craze; her voice, shape and lovely eyes won New York.

MAURICE ARON, a cycling hero, stands beside his victorious wheel. Aron won first prize in the *Evening Telegram's* 1896 parade. His revolutionary one-piece suit was highly praised.

Mayhem, melodrama and Mrs. Fiske

THE vitality of the '90s tumbled about the stage in vigorous vaudeville, blatant burlesque and heart-rending melodrama. Plays called *Dangers of a Great City* and *The Girl I Left Behind Me (right)* were hits. After a run on Broadway they went on tour. By 1900 some 400 touring companies were amusing the country. If the hits were silly enough, and they usually were, Weber and Fields *(below, right)* satirized them in their music-hall routine. William Gillette and James O'Neill acted adventurous roles, and Minnie Maddern Fiske *(below)* upheld the classics. Although Mrs. Astor looked down on actors, the middle classes loved them and the stage boomed in New York and on the road until movies took over.

The theater offers many attractions, not the least of which is the audience.

MISTRESS OF THE STAGE, Mrs. Fiske represents the best of the American theater in the 1890s. A fine tragedienne, she popularized Henrik Ibsen's plays in New York City.

MASTERS OF MAYHEM, Lew Fields and Joe Weber pose ready for action. Their dialect patter and pratfall humor regaled audiences for more than 30 years.

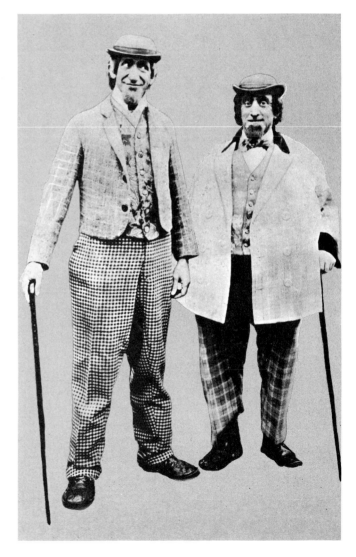

52

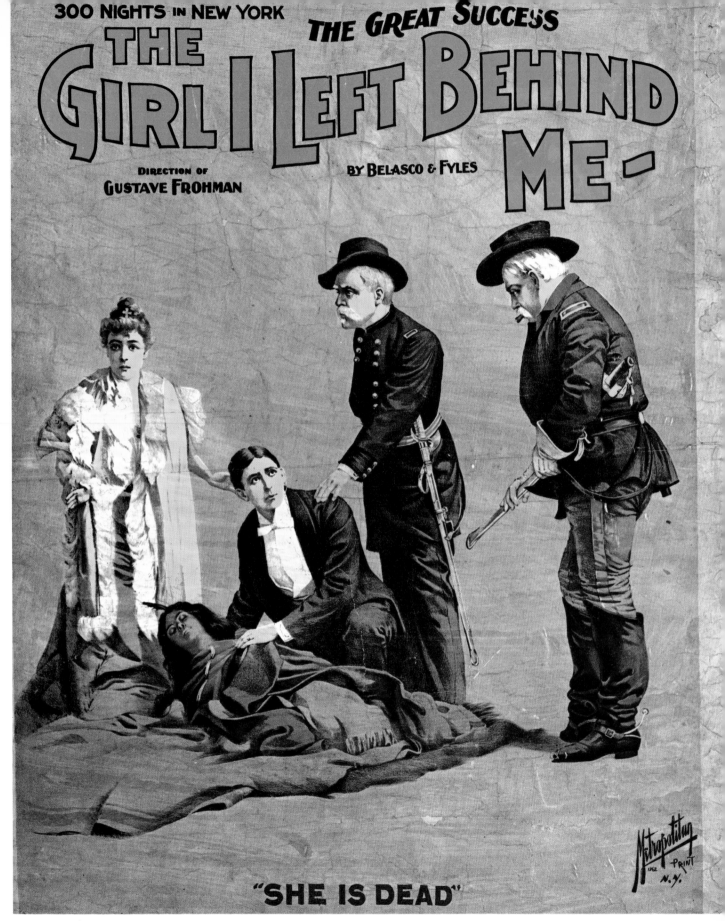

A touching tableau, this is the climax of a melodrama about an Indian uprising. Such plays were sure hits on Broadway and on tour.

New in 1897, Coney Island's Steeplechase Park offers (clockwise) the Canals of Venice, the Scenic Railway, the Giant See-Saw, the Stadium

and a Steeplechase made of iron.

New pleasures, clothes and trolleys for the beaches

A Gibson girl wishes she had more on. The beach dress was daring.

By the '90s, the out-of-doors was opened up. On bicycle, trolley, train or yacht, multitudes of city people traveled out for a Sunday on the beach or at Coney Island's new amusement park *(left)*. Between 1880 and 1890, the country's urban population had grown from 14 to 22 million. And from 1,260 miles of trolley track in 1890, the mileage leaped to nearly 22,000 by 1902. As track was laid, millions of passengers followed. Rides cost only a nickel. Coney Island, which had been a very posh resort where millionaire sportsmen anchored their yachts, became a popular place within reach of the average New Yorker. The island filled up with bathing houses, dance halls, shooting galleries, freak shows and eating houses. Special trolleys brought holiday throngs, and the many amusement parks served, according to *Harper's Weekly,* as "great breathing places for the millions . . . who get little fresh air at home." Seeing the crowds at play, one English observer noted: "The sadness of Puritanism seems to have been shed off."

BRILLIANTLY LIT, trolleys go off on an excursion. Bands played and passengers sang as cool breezes took the edge off the heat. Fares were low. Millions could now afford to leave the city for a holiday.

ELEGANTLY GARBED, a lady cools her ankles in the sea. As much as 10 yards of cloth was used in an outfit. After a decorous dip, bathers could sample the various delights of shoreside entertainment.

"The gentlemen leave the ladies to their tobacco and wine" is the caption of this tongue-in-cheek, but prophetic, Gibson drawing of 1892.

Man's last refuge from woman: the club, the bar

IN the last decade of the 19th Century, American women grew more sporty, ambitious and free than ever before. Famous as hostesses, singers and actresses, they bathed in public, played tennis fearlessly and cycled furiously. By 1900 they even had the vote in four states. Man ran for shelter. Home was no longer safe. There his glittering wife and emancipated daughters outranked him. If he was still young enough, he could tramp across golf links or pursue the wily fox. If portly

and old, a man could retire to his club or a gentleman's bar. In 11 years, 366 secret fraternities were founded. But the future looked bleak. Men ate and drank together as if for the last time. With laurel leaves on their brows, they celebrated their wilting independence (*below*). They clustered in bars like the one in Hoffman House (*opposite*). There, at least, they could meet men —Diamond Jim Brady, Grover Cleveland, Buffalo Bill. Another drink was ordered. Men toasted their past.

A FESTIVE MEAL draws to a stuffy close. Only one man at the plush affair can be identified: Harrison Grey Fiske, husband of the actress, is seated to the right of the white-bearded man.

A MANLY BAR at the Hoffman House boasts famous nudes by the fashionable French painter William Bouguereau. Hoffman's was a noted rendezvous for actors, businessmen and Democrats.

3. A TIDAL WAVE OF IMMIGRANTS

BUT the stranger that dwelleth with you shall be unto you as one born among you, and thou shalt love him as thyself." So the Lord had spoken, through Moses, to the Israelites. The Americans, as the Chosen People of the 19th Century (in their own eyes), took all such commandments with proper seriousness. Moreover, in 1858 Abraham Lincoln had boldly tied together the Republican program for freedom in the territories and the American ideal of proffering to the world's oppressed a gateway to hope. The West, he declared, should be "an outlet for *free white people everywhere*, the world over—in which Hans and Baptiste and Patrick, and all other men from all the world, may find new homes and better their condition in life."

To the generation which took up the nation's business after the Civil War, it was unthinkable to ignore a mandate of Jehovah *and* Lincoln. Yet as the years went by, the fulfillment of the mission of welcome raised perplexing problems. By the '90s, immigration was not only a fact but an issue.

It was a fact first, and an overwhelming one. Before 1860 the largest single year's immigration had been that of 1854, when 427,833 newcomers were numbered. In 1873 that figure was surpassed, as 459,803 entered. In 1881, 669,431 arrived. The next year brought an unprecedented 788,992—not to be exceeded in a single year until 1903. In 1883 the figure dropped to 603,322, but from then through 1899 the annual influx of newcomers only twice dipped below 250,000, and four times it soared above the half-million level.

BENJAMIN HARRISON'S political shrewdness is clear in his opposition to further Chinese immigration while he embraced the Irish newcomers—with their powerful vote.

In all, over 14 million European migrants joined the population between 1860 and 1900. (Some 18 million were to follow between 1900 and 1930.) In 1900 the ratio of natives to foreign-born—6 to 1—was approximately what it had been 40 years earlier, but the greater mass and concentration of the immigrant population made the newcomers, in some ways, more noticeable than they had been in the past.

About 15 million Americans at the opening of the 20th Century had at least one parent born abroad. That fact had great emotional and cultural significance in the daily lives of the younger generation. Almost every third person in the land—counting both the foreign-born and their immediate descendants—was touched by the pride and pathos of alienation and transplantation.

It was an age of steam and of swift movement against wind and tide, an age which could uproot and reroot entire peoples in a generation. The 14,-061,192 Europeans who came to the United States from 1860 to 1900 made up a total greater than the entire population of some small European nations today. A single generation sufficed to move the equivalent of an entire nationality a quarter of the way around the globe to new homes.

IF the steam engine furnished the means of emigration, it also helped create the reasons for it. When rails across the prairies and steamships across the Atlantic brought Nebraska wheat to undersell Bohemian or German wheat in Europe itself, Bohemian and German farmers felt a dreadful pinch. One way of easing it was to move themselves to Nebraska soils. When estate managers in Central Europe introduced modern harvesting machinery, unskilled farm laborers found their future closed—and listened with new interest to stories of golden America, especially as the New World seemed sparsely populated in comparison with increasingly crowded Europe. When times were hard, British textile workers, German coal miners and Belgian factory hands remembered what they had heard and read of marvelous places called Fall River and Buffalo and Toledo, where good jobs might be had. Southern Italy in the 1880s and 1890s was a region of worn-out soils and absentee-owned estates, whose landlords seldom used their meager revenues to improve their holdings. The peasants of the south were more than ready to exchange endless hunger for whatever a new world might offer.

Man's political sensitivity (and callousness) helped too. Many a peasant fled from a village raked over once too often by the conscription gangs or an occupying enemy or particularly-thorough tax gatherers. In Eastern Europe the multinational empires established by Turkey and Austria were slowly being dissolved by the acids of nationalism. As middle-class Magyars, Croats, Greeks, Serbs, Slovaks, Poles, Bohemians and Rumanians struggled against their imperial masters, the wave of revolts and repressions rose. Many an intellectual from Central or Eastern Europe crossed the border just ahead of the police. Nationalism also made life hard, and exile, therefore, a reasonable alternative for minority groups. Persecution of Jews in Russia from 1881 through the early 20th Century kept pace with rising Pan-Slavic feeling. Goodly numbers of German Catholics were uneasy inside a German empire established in 1871 under the dominance of non-Catholic Prussia.

So they stirred and reached out, and human tides moved westward. It was said that Americans urged them on—railroads looking for customers for their land, contractors rounding up men for the mill and the mine, new Western

This cartoon, published in "Leslie's Weekly" in 1888, shows the reaction to unrestricted immigration by old-time Americans. The older stocks felt that they were the only true Yankees and they objected to the heavy influx of many races and nationalities. Most newcomers, though proud to be American, fed opposition by clinging to their native language and customs.

states eager for heads to count and hands to build. And all this was partly true. The railroads—in particular the land-grant lines—did provide immigrant trains and they did put up handbills in steamship offices and American consulates abroad advertising lands for sale on easy terms. While the railroads wanted to sell land, they were equally anxious to create traffic. Jim Hill's Great Northern, a line with no land grant, carried Swedes and Norwegians westward from St. Paul in boxlike "Zulu cars," helped to settle them and even taught them how to farm on the Northern prairies.

Recruiting agents did meet ships at the dock; sometimes they were state agents, sometimes independent operators who spoke foreign languages and specialized in assembling gangs of Greek or Italian workers to deliver to employers. But they were intercepting a stream already in motion. The railroad land salesman, the steamship ticket agent and the work-gang boss (or *padrone*, as some immigrants called him) buttonholed the traveler after he had decided to leave Europe, either at an embarkation point or when he landed in the United States. For when all was said and done, it was the immigrant's own yearning which sent him out into the world on a long, lonely road—against the tug of his own fears of the new, his own loyalties to the old.

The '60s and '70s saw thousands of Norwegian, Swedish and German immigrants swept into the aching, if fertile, solitudes of the Northern plains. Russian-German Mennonites—a religious sect stubbornly determined to bear no arms, swear no oaths and spurn worldly vanities of a corrupt world—came to Kansas in great numbers in the '70s, fleeing the persecution of a hostile czar. Bohemians, like the Shimerdas of Willa Cather's *My Antonia*, took up life on Nebraska prairies.

Flung out over sprawling farms, many immigrants missed the warmth and the intimacy of their village lives. Some broke, some were coarsened. Some became triumphantly American as Olsens and Svensons and Shimerdas completed the frontier-breaking process begun long before by Boones, Lincolns and Jacksons.

B Y the '90s the bulk of immigration was heading for the cities. This was not entirely by predilection: The newcomers were simply making the same adjustment that native Americans were making as the good lands of the West were taken up. Some European peasants did manage to break into agriculture, though not always on the prairies. The Polish or Portuguese or Italian raiser of vegetables, fruit and tobacco began to appear in numbers which increased rapidly after 1900, both in California and on the Eastern Seaboard from New England southward as far as Delaware.

But most, by choice or need, went to the factory or the mine. In 1875 Andrew Carnegie's production chief, William Jones, was praising the virtues of Germans, Irish and Swedes (with a leaven of "buckwheats," or American country boys) as the "most effective and tractable force" for uninterrupted steelmaking. By 1900 steel-mill labor also included Poles, Hungarians, Russians, Lithuanians, Bohemians, Slovaks and Italians. A report on the coal industry in 1901 noted that in the anthracite coal fields alone, there were 100,000 Slavs; and the Slavic-born percentage in some individual mines ran as high as 7 out of 10.

In New York City during the '90s, thousands of Russian Jews huddled in tenement rooms, squinting as they sewed clothing contracted out to them by

A GREATHEARTED WELCOME

TO THE PROMISED LAND

Inscribed on a plaque at the Statue of Liberty, this sonnet by Emma Lazarus reflects an early American attitude toward immigration. The originally generous policy has, however, been watered down by a discriminatory quota system based on ancient prejudices that favor immigrants from Northern Europe.

Not like the brazen giant of Greek fame,
With conquering limbs astride from land to land;
Here at our sea-washed, sunset gates shall stand
A mighty woman with a torch, whose flame
Is the imprisoned lightning, and her name
Mother of Exiles. From her beacon-hand
Glows world-wide welcome, her mild eyes command
The air-bridged harbor that twin-cities frame.
"Keep, ancient lands, your storied pomp!" cries she
With silent lips. "Give me your tired, your poor,
Your huddled masses yearning to breathe free,
The wretched refuse of your teeming shore,
Send these, the homeless, tempest-tost to me;
I lift my lamp beside the golden door!"

small-scale manufacturers. German and Bohemian cigarmakers also worked at home, in unhealthful conditions, though Cigarmakers' Union officials like Adolph Strasser and Samuel Gompers fought to stamp out the practice by law.

New York was especially cosmopolitan in its population. Gompers noted the presence of former "soldiers from the red-shirted army of Garibaldi; German 'forty-eighters,' English Chartists . . . the *carbonari* of Italy; the home-rulers of Ireland; revolutionaries from Denmark, Austria, Russia." Reporter Jacob Riis in 1890 observed that the Italians in New York already dominated the corner fruit stands and bootblacking shops, while the Chinese were in "almost exclusive possession of the laundry business." A map of the city, with colors indicating the location of various groups, said Riis, would "show more stripes than on the skin of a zebra, and more colors than any rainbow"—from solid patches for large German, Irish, Russian-Jewish, Italian and black neighborhoods, to "dots and dashes of color here and there . . . where the Finnish sailors worship their *djumala* (God), the Greek pedlers the ancient name of their race, and the Swiss the goddess of thrift."

A NATION OF VILLAGERS MOVING TO THE CITIES

Two factors accounted for the phenomenal growth of U.S. cities between 1870 (size shown in black) and 1900 (in brown): Of the 10 million immigrants who arrived in these years, six million settled in urban areas. In addition, countless farm laborers displaced by mechanization took jobs in booming city-based industries. Total population grew almost 100 per cent to 75 million, but urban growth was well over 200 per cent. Chicago's expansion led the field—an astounding 500 per cent to 1.7 million. And Denver, under 5,000 in 1870, had more than 100,000 people by 1900.

NEW YORK was not the only Babel in the nation. In the 1890s Chicago had more Germans than any cities in the German Empire except Berlin and Hamburg, more Swedes than any Swedish cities except Stockholm and Göteborg, more Norwegians than any places save Oslo and Bergen. Cleveland in 1890 had 100,000 foreign-born, Detroit 80,000, Minneapolis 60,000.

Outside the major cities, Poles and Lithuanians, Greeks and Syrians,

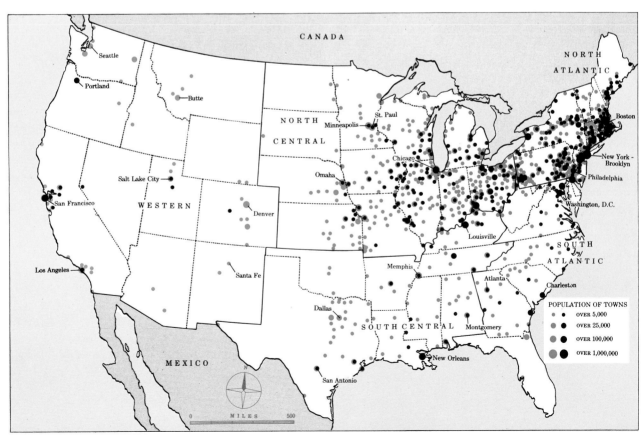

French-Canadians and Portuguese spun yarn in Paterson and Lowell, loaded coal cars in Scranton, packed pork in Kansas City. By 1900 immigrants furnished a goodly proportion of the work force in any industry that relied on unskilled labor. There were, of course, specially skilled immigrant groups, like Czech glass blowers or German musical-instrument makers, that broke with the stereotype of the willing but untrained immigrant.

In the towns where immigrant workers clustered, many of the tailors, grocers, undertakers and priests tended to be of immigrant stock too. So by 1890, according to one somewhat hostile observer, "the people of the free States became divided into classes. . . natives and foreigners."

The division did not necessarily have to be a sharp one. A society can choose to make much or little of the distinction between the home-born and the newly joined member. Americans had made little of the difference for most of their history. In the '80s and '90s, however, some of them shifted to a new tack—of opposition to the "alien."

The shift came simultaneously with a change in the major geographic sources of immigration. The newcomers from 1885 onward continued with the blasting, shoveling, plowing and machine tending which had always made up the immigrant's mighty contribution to the nation's growth. But now their already-burdensome environment bristled with the challenge of "nativism."

From the beginning, America had welcomed the adventurer who brought skill, muscle or capital to a land in great need of them. Yet behind the reality of that open-armed reception, there was always the instinctive distrust of the

A PATCHWORK OF NATIVE AND FOREIGN-BORN

This map shows the ratio, by area, of foreign-born and native Americans in 1900. Some 85 per cent of the immigrants settled in the increasingly urbanized North Atlantic and North Central states. Foreign-born groups also loomed large in sparsely populated border areas like the Northeast, with its Canadians; the Northern Plains, where Scandinavians and Canadians clustered; and the Southwest and Far West, home of many Mexicans and Chinese. The mainly agricultural South Atlantic and South Central areas drew a tiny percentage of the new Americans.

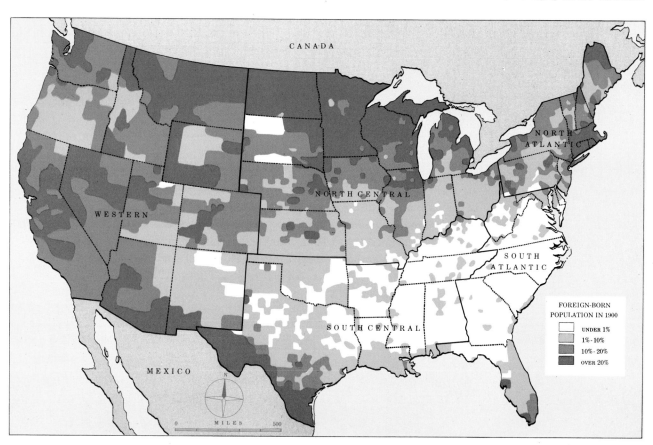

FOREIGN-BORN
POPULATION IN 1900

UNDER 1%
1% - 10%
10% - 20%
OVER 20%

stranger. As a rule, that suspicion was not an important force in American politics. Nevertheless it did blaze forth at times—and particularly when the nation itself seemed under threat.

In times of peril it became, for some, more urgent than ever to define and protect—by hostility to outsiders—what was peculiarly American. The greatest pre-Civil War outburst of nativism took place during the heyday of the foreigner-and-Catholic-hating American, or Know-Nothing, party. That was in the '50s, when political passions flowed hot as lava and finally melted the links of union. After the Civil War, nativism subsided in the upsurge of growth.

As the '80s ended, anxiety once more darkened the horizon. The apparently limitless lands of the West were disappearing; the trust was riding high. Capital and labor were locked in battle. Old religious faiths were on the defensive. Despite the swelling magnificence of the new America's physical achievement, fear nibbled at the edge of self-confidence. Perhaps American ideals were being misshapen and distorted in the very midst of success.

This was the precise point at which immigration not only grew in size, but changed in nature. Until roughly 1890, most of those entering the United States came from the British Isles, Germany and the Scandinavian countries. Soon after, migrants from Southern and Eastern Europe began to predominate. They were 18.3 per cent of the total immigration in the '80s, but 52.8 per cent in the '90s. In the first decade of the 20th Century, they made up 71.9 per cent of the more than eight million new arrivals.

At best, it would have taken time for old-stock Americans to become accustomed to new faces and new accents. But the times were turbulent, and there was an additional barrier to acceptance of newcomers in the form of a growing celebration of Anglo-Saxon virtues. Strictly speaking, an Anglo-Saxon was someone descended from the peoples who made up the historic population of Great Britain. American leaders, from colonial days, had been drawn largely from that stock, and took justifiable pride in its achievements.

SUCH pride did not *necessarily* go hand in hand with contempt for other peoples (except Negroes) until the '80s, when the rising vogue of Darwinism gave some respectability to a number of questionable views. Among them was the notion that the different "races" of mankind had certain hereditary intellectual and social characteristics that determined their position in the struggle for survival. A conclusion was drawn that the achievements of culturally advanced nations—most notably Great Britain and America—were due to their unchangeable "racial" bent for progress and self-government. The corollary, obviously, was that "backward" nations owed their problems of illiteracy and misery to the natural inferiority of their hereditary strain.

This doctrine served as a superb rationalization for British and American empire-builders, from Alabama to Burma, who were dominating nonwhite peoples. And European nations carving out colonial domains furnished their own variants of the doctrine without the Anglo-Saxon trappings.

It remained for certain Americans, however, to turn the belief in Anglo-Saxon superiority into a weapon against some continental Europeans, especially those who were knocking for admission to the United States after 1890. Out of the amalgam of Anglo-Saxon pride, the misapplication of Darwinian theory to human history, and the tensions of industrial America grew the legend of the "old" and the "new" immigration.

Immigrants who settled in the Nebraska plains found that chunks of grass-tufted sod made the handiest building material. Sod houses could be built for as little as five dollars. They were a drab and dusty gray in dry weather, but weeds, morning-glories and prairie roses sprouted from rooftops and walls when the rains came. Some 19th Century sod houses still stand.

Prior to 1880, the story went, there had been a voluntary immigration to the United States, made up mostly of British, Scandinavian, German and Irish peoples. This "old" migration, from Northern and Western Europe, was sturdy, pioneering and permanent. In the words of a 1910 report, the old immigrants "mingled freely with the native Americans and were quickly assimilated." But the new immigration was different.

The new immigrant—the Greek, the Pole, the Serb, the Hungarian, the Italian—was considered another breed. A whole mythology was created to explain him. He had not come wholly on his own, but had been corralled by a steamship line or a labor recruiter. He did not bring his family with him. He willingly worked for starvation wages, huddled in slums which no native American could tolerate, paid fewer taxes than the native, took a larger share of public charity and committed a greater share of the crimes. He was often a bird of passage, making a stake in the United States and then returning home. Or, if he stayed long enough to acquire citizenship papers, he sold his vote to politicians for the cheapest of handouts. He was a radical. Had it not been anarchists, speaking a foreign tongue, whose propaganda lit the fuse of the Haymarket explosion? He was, in short, unassimilable, and he threatened to break down American civilization.

A HISTORY written nowadays need not concern itself with disproving these charges, though it should be mentioned that they were the basis of the quota system that underlay immigration laws until 1968; these laws were heavily weighted against the countries of the Central European and Mediterranean area. It should be noted, however, that the indictment of the new immigrants was stated in the most general terms of comparison between the old and new waves of immigrants. The charges failed to take account of the more significant differences between individual nationality groups. The Bohemians, merely to cite one example, had almost no illiteracy, despite the nativist's conclusion that the new immigration, as a whole, was undereducated.

More important, the making of distinctions between two arbitrarily defined categories of immigrants—oldtimers and recent arrivals—was inherently unfair. Those who had been longer in America had had years to move up the economic and social ladder. Literacy, family, property, the will and power to contribute to the larger community—these had come only with time to the older immigrants, as they would come, in time, to the newer group.

Yet there were Americans in the '90s who deeply believed in the nativist legend and in its fearful implications. New anxieties were nourished by old prejudices. The immigration of the '80s and '90s was heavily Roman Catholic, and anti-Catholicism had a history in America which went back to the Puritan settlers who had fled the "Romish idolatry" of Charles I. In Clinton, Iowa, in 1887, there was formed an anti-Catholic organization known as the American Protective Association. Within a decade it was declining rapidly. But in 1894 it was claiming a million members whose suspicions of the city, the new immigrant and the Pope fused into one.

The new immigration also contained large numbers of Jews, and anti-Semitism had its American adherents. Despite a general record of acceptance of Jews, the United States contained those who saw in every successful Jew a grasping Shylock, and in every impoverished Russian or Polish Jew of the new immigration an unassimilable outlander.

Early in this century, there were more Italians living in New York City than there were in Rome. Among this group were skilled craftsmen like the "Italian Image-Maker" shown in this 1869 drawing. So many "Little Italys" grew up in major American cities that to claim Italian ancestry became a great advantage for politicians making Columbus Day speeches.

65

During his 37 years of service in the House and the Senate, Henry Cabot Lodge was rarely on the side of reform; one exception was his defense of the civil service laws. More characteristic was his ruthless fight against unrestricted immigration in which he demonstrated the stubborn-mindedness he later used more successfully in opposing the League of Nations.

One group seemed, indeed, to have a legitimate grievance against the new arrivals. This was the working class, which suffered from the repeated use of imported immigrant strikebreakers. Labor leaders sometimes found it difficult to recognize that the immigrant who accepted such work in preference to starvation was as much a victim as the native worker.

Labor's discontent with the post-Civil War tide of immigration had first flared up on the West Coast against the Chinese. They were an obvious target. They had come to California by the thousands in the '60s and '70s. Mostly they were employed by the railroads as pick-and-shovel workers, but they took whatever jobs—and whatever dregs of farmland and mining claim—white men would allow them. They were stolid under hardship and visibly different in a multitude of small ways: in their exotic foods like dried cuttlefish, in their pigtails, in their language, in a hundred colorful customs. The white workingmen hated them as the ultimate in "coolie" competition, and the white "respectable" classes rolled eyes in horror at their fondness for gambling, their alleged addiction to opium and their "heathen" worship.

Together, lower- and middle-class Californians overcame the objections of many employers and pressed through restrictive legislation, first in their own state, and then—aided by other such groups in the nation—in Congress. In 1882 the Chinese Exclusion Act stopped the immigration of Chinese laborers for 10 years, a prohibition later renewed. Three years later, labor spokesmen took additional satisfaction from the passage of the Foran Act, which prohibited the signing of contract workers abroad. It was a feeble victory. Crews of strikebreakers could still be rounded up in immigrant boardinghouses in American ports.

In the 1890s a new group entered the nativistic fold, quite distinct from the suspicious Midwestern farmers or the protective spokesmen for labor. Thomas Bailey Aldrich, a decorous writer and versifier of the period, was a member of the nativist group. For a time editor of the *Atlantic*, spearhead of the era's gentility, Aldrich warned:

> Wide open and unguarded stand our gates,
> And through them presses a wild motley throng—
> Men from the Volga and the Tartar steppes,
> Featureless figures from the Hoang-Ho,
> Malayan, Scythian, Teuton, Kelt, and Slav,
> Flying the Old World's poverty and scorn;
> These bringing with them unknown gods and rites,
> Those, tiger passions, here to stretch their claws....
> O Liberty, white Goddess! is it well
> To leave the gates unguarded?...
> Have a care
> Lest from thy brow the clustered stars be torn
> And trampled in the dust.

Aldrich was in elite company, for the new group consisted primarily of New Englanders of ancient stock and pedigree—men like evolutionist John Fiske; Massachusetts Senator Henry Cabot Lodge; Henry and Brooks Adams, the bright and morose brothers who never forgot that they were grandsons of a President; and Francis A. Walker, onetime Union general, well-known economist and president of the Massachusetts Institute of Technology.

These, and others like them, belonged to old families. They had seen politics pass into the hands of bosses, and business pass into the hands of hustling grabbers whose wealth did not conceal bad breeding. They felt out of place in the new America, and it was no surprise that they turned on the proletarian immigrant with genteel fury. Fiske explained that the new immigration came from countries "where the grade of civilization and the general standard of living is very low." Walker said it was drawn from "beaten races; representing the worst failures in the struggle for existence."

To help repulse the "beaten races," Yankee bluebloods formed the Immigration Restriction League in 1894. Two years later in Washington, Senator Lodge introduced a bill to restrict admission to literate aliens, explaining frankly that the test would "bear most heavily upon the Italians, Russians, Poles, Hungarians, Greeks and Asiatics . . . races . . . who are the most alien to the great body of the people of the United States."

The bill passed but was vetoed by Grover Cleveland with characteristic directness. The big and blunt Democratic President insisted that America owed much to the "assimilation and thrift of sturdy and patriotic adopted citizens," and in any case, violence and disorder did not "originate with illiterate laborers. They are rather the victims of an educated agitator." It was like Cleveland to try to catch both restrictionists and radicals with one swing of his fist. Despite his veto the restrictive forces continued their campaign as the century ended, but they seemed to be making little headway in halting the human flow.

Charles Proteus Steinmetz, a brilliant electrical engineer, left Germany in 1882 because he feared arrest for his political views. He was one of many immigrants (like Albert Einstein, Andrew Carnegie, Hideyo Noguchi) who enriched life in this country. After becoming an American citizen, he wrote to a friend that "there is nothing to be got in Europe, everything here."

A<small>ND</small> what of the immigrant himself, who was the subject of the debate? He did his best to find his bearings in the New World. Sometimes he was an outstanding success. The pride of nationality groups has carefully preserved the records of those who attained the heights in the professional and social worlds. If taste runs to stories of financial success, there is the saga of Henry Villard, German-born, at the age of 20 peddling books and real estate in his adopted Illinois and struggling to master English—and at 55 chairman of the board of Northern Pacific, founder of the Edison General Electric Company and owner of the New York *Post*.

If such accounts seem to pay too much attention to the wealthy, there is the story of Daniel De Leon. He was born in the Dutch West Indies, educated in Europe and reached the United States in the early '70s. He attended law school, lectured at Columbia University and then was caught up in social agitation. He became a leader of the Socialist Labor party and founded the short-lived Socialist Trade and Labor Alliance. Among his enemies was Samuel Gompers, the English-born descendant of Dutch Jews who made the American Federation of Labor the bedrock of the American labor movement.

Should millionaires and socialists and labor leaders fail to hold the interest of any reader of the immigrant saga, there are the wonderful stories about scientists. Michael Idvor Pupin, a Serb, arrived in the United States in 1874 with a red fez on his head and five cents in his pocket. Half a century later he won the Pulitzer Prize for an autobiography which told how he rose to become a brilliant electrophysicist at Columbia. Charles Proteus Steinmetz, a refugee from German Chancellor Otto von Bismarck's anti-Socialist laws, went to work for the General Electric Company in 1892. He sat in his laboratory for years, a hunchbacked little genius with a cigar in his mouth, filling sheets of paper with calculations that sent alternating current pulsing through thousands of miles of wire and lit up hundreds of cities and villages like stars.

If the pages are turned to the arts, it is almost impossible to find a symphony conductor in the United States before World War II who was not foreign-born. The operetta king of the 20th Century's opening years was Victor Herbert, born in Ireland. Herbert's successor, as perhaps the best-known, unashamedly popular balladeer of America, was born in Russia under the name of Isidore Baline. He is more recognizable as Irving Berlin. "God Bless America," Berlin's hymn to his adopted country, came to the United States (as did so many other contributions to American culture) via the immigrant steamer.

Under the ironic title "Live and Let Live in Russia," this "Harper's Weekly" cartoon carried the caption "Your money, Jew, or your life!" From their free land of limitless opportunity, 19th Century Americans viewed the violent persecutions of Russian Jews with deep revulsion. Yet American nativist movements opposed immigration of the world's oppressed.

STORIES like these are part of the literature of ancestor worship among immigrant groups. But there is an infinite variety of human interest in the untold tales of the average immigrant. There was the arrival in New York, with the figure of the Statue of Liberty, erected in 1886, visible all up the harbor. Then there was the confusion of landing at Castle Garden— or, after 1892, on Ellis Island. There were the probings of the medical examiners, the stumbling onto the pier, the search for relatives, the stammering questions asked of hurrying strangers—"Vere iss train, Pittsboig?"

There were other welcomes—from the boardinghouse keeper, the *padrone*, the railway ticket seller. And then more journeyings, and at the end the construction camp, the tenement house, the painful groping for perception among shouts, curses, orders, rumors. The familiar world of village and church or synagogue gave way to a brick-and-stone bedlam, a prairie emptiness. It took time to re-establish roots, learn the feel of job and home, join hands with those of the old faith and the old ways. In time one could make some kind of life that embraced the old and the new.

A man could read the Polish or Bohemian newspaper, worship in a church filled with other Ukrainians or Hungarians, even find others with whom to celebrate the old-country holidays—in the Sons of Italy, or the Polish National Alliance. A man could make a life that gave him a feeling of being a bit less strange—except that he could not reach out and hold his children within the halfway house. Gradually he became aware that they spoke in a different idiom; moved to a different rhythm; looked on him with contempt, or pity, or at best from across a gulf that never could be bridged.

The children could make the full transition to the New World. On the farm they learned to do the chores, keep the accounts and do what Americans did in town on Saturdays. And in the city they found their way around among the crowded streets of little Italy or little Poland—playing their games among the pushcart wheels, dodging from stoop to stoop, chirping brightly in a patois of foreign language and English about baseball, swallowing their breakfast and rushing off to the strange public school.

As they grew older they went different ways. Some learned to practice the arts of the precinct worker, whose duties were so essential to the lost and bewildered immigrant. (A marvelous man, the precinct worker, for finding a job, getting a peddler's license from a mysterious officialdom, raising money for uniforms for the parish football team.) Some immigrant children even became political bosses. Others combined work at their jobs with union activity, made speeches, posted handbills, found meaning to life in what they called the workers' struggle. Some, in the cities again, went to classes in the settlement house or at the school, fought their way up the educational ladder and became doctors, lawyers, teachers, to the bemusement and joy of their parents. Some never got quite that high: They became keepers of candy stores, tailor shops and groceries like those of their fathers. And a few matriculated in pool halls, learned things not taught in Americanism classes and graduated into crime.

Whatever the children did, they felt that they were Americans. The vitality of the new country was theirs. Their story is generally one set in the 20th Century, when they grew to maturity, but even by the '90s they knew this was their home, whatever the Immigration Restriction League might say. In the 1770s a French veteran of Montcalm's army living in North America had written that "in this great American asylum, the poor of Europe have by some means met together" and "melted into a new race of men, whose labors and posterity will one day cause great changes in the world." More than a century after J. Hector St. John Crèvecoeur wrote those words, other newcomers were fulfilling his prediction.

In the '90s in Boston, there lived a dark-eyed young Jewish girl only just arrived from Polotzk, in Russia. In her public school, as she was later to recall in her writings, Mary Antin was introduced to an American past which, miraculously, was hers. "This George Washington, who died long before I was born," she discovered, "was like a king in greatness, and he and I were Fellow Citizens." In a republic which made Mary Antin, child of the formal ghetto of Polotzk and the informal ghetto of a Boston slum, a Fellow Citizen of George Washington, there was hope. "I strove to conduct myself," she recalled, "as befitted a Fellow Citizen."

Thousands of other young immigrants would make the same discovery and the same resolve. And as they did, Mary Antin perceived, the dream of America as the asylum of the world and the home of a new race of men would be carried on. She told the old-stock Americans to keep an eye on those newcomers. "What if the creature with the untidy beard carries in his bosom his citizenship papers? What if the cross-legged tailor is supporting a boy in college who is one day going to mend your state constitution for you? What if the ragpicker's daughters are hastening over the ocean to teach your children in the public schools?"

Such questions were meant to carry their own answer. The mood of multitudes of immigrants, who had voluntarily torn themselves up by the roots in search of a fresher world, was confidence. If their confidence was somewhat shaken by harsh experience, that of their children was unshakably strong—and was, in addition, one of the surest bonds uniting them with the mainstream of American thinking.

As immigrant and nativist confronted each other in hostility, still one more thread of antagonism was stretched on the loom of American history. In one more way, the values of Washington's and Jefferson's and Jackson's and Lincoln's America were to be put to the test. Like industrialization, the trust, the freed Negro—like all of them, the immigrant was to confront America with troublesome problems arising out of the conflict between ideals and practice. The problems had to be accepted as existing in many areas before they could be eased by moving practice and ideals closer together. The immigrant was simply one more question mark posed in the turbulent '90s.

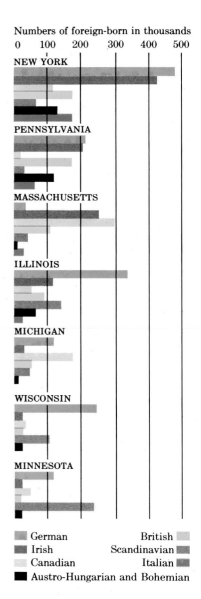

Numbers of foreign-born in thousands

German — British
Irish — Scandinavian
Canadian — Italian
Austro-Hungarian and Bohemian

IMMIGRANT ENCLAVES IN THE NEW WORLD

In 1900, 6.3 million of the 10.3 million foreign-born in the U.S. lived in seven states (above). Germans formed 25.7 per cent of the U.S. total; 15.6 per cent were Irish, 11.4 per cent Canadian, 11.3 per cent British, 10.3 per cent Scandinavian, 5.6 per cent Austro-Hungarian-Bohemian and 4.7 per cent Italian. (The great exodus from Eastern Europe of the late 19th Century is not reflected here.) In 1900 New York City was truly the "great melting pot": it had 1.3 million foreign-born. This was 36.7 per cent of the city population, 12.3 per cent of America's foreign-born.

A cheerless start for a new life

As the avalanche of immigrants smashed into American cities, the squeeze fell heavily on the children. Adults had made the difficult and painful decision to migrate. But children crossed the ocean willy-nilly, got a glimpse of the Statue of Liberty *(below)* and then were swallowed up by the suffocating world of the tenements. Toward the turn of the century the population density in one part of lower Manhattan was nearly 1,000 persons per acre, and the island was the most crowded spot on earth. Many apartments housed nine people per room; in one downtown block, there were 2,781 persons. Newly arrived children, confined to verminous firetraps, soon competed for space with American-born brothers and sisters. Later, writers of nostalgic memoirs might rhapsodize about the color and variety of slum life, but the noise and stench and abrasion of daily living could bring despair even to the eyes of a small boy *(opposite)*.

Two photographers made most of the pictures on these pages: Danish-born Jacob Riis, whose camera supplied incontrovertible evidence for his blazing exposés of slum conditions, and Lewis Hine of Wisconsin, who devoted himself to documenting the conditions among immigrants and child laborers. These two men's visual records mirror the hard life most new Americans had to face.

Immigrants of all ages, entering New York harbor in 1887, gaze at the new Statue of Liberty. Some of them look eager, some almost fearful.

A TENEMENT WINDOW provides a frame for a portrait of a wistful child. At one time or another, millions of immigrants lived in similar quarters, whose common features included rick-ety construction, too few fire escapes, inadequate or stopped-up plumbing, poor light. These miserable homes could convert America's vaunted freedom into a child's vision of the Inferno.

Humanity at close quarters

IMMIGRANT slum existence was communal with a vengeance. Indoors, a youngster could hardly move without stepping on someone else, and if sent out to play he fared little better. Jacob Riis wrote of "dark hallways and filthy cellars, crowded . . . with dirty children." He warned the prospective visitor to take care: "The hall is dark and you might stumble over the children pitching pennies back there." Boys and girls clustered on stoops

Areas where children in lower Manhattan played around 1900 include (left to right) a sunless court off a tenement building, the swarming

and fire escapes, in wash-hung courts and trash-laden alleys *(below, right)*, even near open privies.

Along the sidewalks swirled the tides of the city life. The streets were alive with men and women talking, shouting, bargaining in a dozen tongues *(below, center)*. For blocks, lower Manhattan was an odorous open-air marketplace where storekeepers competed with push-carts, wagons and temporary stands offering every kind of article, fresh and otherwise. Riis cited "bandanas and tin cups at two cents, peaches at a cent a quart, 'damaged' eggs for a song." Children on their own errands slipped through the turmoil like eels. For some boys the street was the locale of their real home: the gang that thrived on petty thievery. But the slums produced musicians and scientists along with criminals. Each in his own way had fled the pressures of poverty and people.

tunnel of Orchard Street and a dark, narrow back alley with what could be members of a street gang posed behind a row of ash cans.

ALL ALONE in a slum hallway, a grave youngster evokes Riis's comment on a water pump shared by many tenants: "Hear the pump squeak! It is the lullaby of tenement-house babes."

Poignant alternatives: Sweated labor or desertion

IMMIGRANT parents toiling 72 or more hours a week for subsistence had scant time to give to their children's welfare, and day nurseries were almost unknown before the turn of the century. Very young boys and girls might be left alone *(left)* or in the care of only slightly older sisters *(opposite)*. Some children were simply abandoned. Riis described one foundling whose parent had written on a slip of paper: "Take care of Johnny, for God's sake. I cannot." By 1889 the 37-year-old Children's Aid Society, Riis noted, had sheltered some 300,000 "outcast, homeless and orphaned children."

One way to cope with extra mouths was to make them feed themselves through piecework done at home. In New York this usually meant making garments, cigars or artificial flowers *(below)*. Monotonous, unsanitary indoor work was no substitute for play, but it was notably better than being turned out into the street to starve.

WORKING WITH MOTHER, children help make paper roses for 20 cents a gross, thus earning two to three dollars a week. Many families took in lodgers to eke out miserable incomes.

HELD BY HER SISTER, this tenement toddler *(opposite)* is in relatively safe hands. A child herself, the older girl has had to telescope her own youth to help her overburdened parents.

74

A STREET VENDOR lugging a basket sells matches and flypaper. Other street jobs included those of newsboy and messenger.

A FACTORY HAND aged about 10 poses for his picture. In 1904 only 17 states had set a minimum age of 14 for factory workers.

COAL MINERS in Pennsylvania are pictured during midday meal break. None is older than 12, but they got their jobs—separating bits of stone from the coal—by claiming to be 14, the legal minimum age.

Sidewalk scavengers work over rubbish baskets for articles that might bring a few cents from some co-operative dealer in second-hand goods.

The disgraceful spectacle of exploited children

THE long, dishonorable history of child labor in America has shown few uglier faces than it did to the offspring of turn-of-the-century immigrants. For 100 years or more, boys and girls had worked in mills, mines and factories. Children were numerous, available and cheap, and work "kept the youngsters out of mischief." The 1900 census showed some 790,000 working children aged 10 to 13, and 960,000 aged 14 to 15—an increase of a million in the 10 to 15 bracket since 1870. It was taken almost for granted that working-class children would go to work as soon as a job was available, with no concessions on hours (10 to 12 a day or night) because of age.

Immigrant children quickly found their places in the sordid ranks of child labor. The younger ones toiled at home on piecework for the "sweated" trades. Driven by need, parents set even babies of three years to work on the simpler tasks, such as straightening tobacco leaves. Four-year-olds helped with the making of artificial flowers. There is a confirmed report of a girl of seven who had sat cross-legged for four years pulling basting threads from garments. As a result, her legs had become paralyzed. Older children worked on the streets or in factories. In the coal fields they picked slate from swiftly moving streams of coal *(opposite)*. The result appears in the drawn, prematurely aged faces seen on these pages, almost all photographed by Lewis Hine's camera.

PLANNED PLAY FACILITIES at New York's pioneering Hudson-bank Playground (opened in 1898) give immigrant youngsters healthy recreation. By 1910 over 150 cities had playgrounds.

A PATRIOTIC DISPLAY of American flags on this tenement fire escape illustrates how quickly immigrants learned to express a Pilgrim's pride in the land they had adopted as their own.

CHILDREN SALUTING the flag held by a fellow pupil stand at attention in a New York industrial school in 1892. All across America, schools took the lead in turning aliens into citizens.

The rocky but certain road to Americanization

ANY immigrant of the late 19th Century who meant to better himself knew the importance of "becoming American." On the other hand, in the harsh atmosphere of the new country, his best chance for survival was through association with immigrants from his native country or village. But if he cautiously stayed among his own kind, he might never even learn English.

His children were more flexible. They could take advantage of the opportunities offered by a growing number of schools, settlement houses and playgrounds *(left)*. Americanization followed almost, but not quite, auto-

matically as they took part in these neighborhood programs. The process was far from painless. It drove a wedge between the generations and undermined the immigrant community. Immigrant parents watched with mingled pride and dismay as their children discarded the tongue of their fathers, questioned the tenets of their ancestral faith and fought their way up, spurning the sweatshop wages for which their fathers had toiled. The promise persisted, the words of "America" rose many-accented but strong, and in a generation the immigrant child had turned into an American.

Latter-day pioneer family

Transfixed in the glare of flash powder, this tenement family could be any of the thousands from all over Europe that landed in New York during the flood tide of immigration. It is a big family—parents, 10 children, grandmother—and the bare floor, meager possessions and ill-fitting clothes testify to an income

just about adequate for daily demands. Among its few furnishings, two are indispensable: the coal stove, used both for cooking and heating the apartment, and the alarm clock that gets Father off to work (and some of the children to school) on time. At the moment, the family has the basic job of providing its members a haven of warmth and familiarity in a city of crowding strangers. Before long one child, then another, will go out to see for himself whether America is still the land of opportunity. Finally all will be gone and the family's job will be finished—and the children no longer will be immigrants.

4. PANIC
AND CRISIS:
1893-1896

ALL through the winter of 1892-1893, half-frozen workmen were busy on an empty-looking stretch of beach and bog that edged Lake Michigan, just south of Chicago. They were building a new wonderland—the World's Columbian Exposition of 1893. By opening day, May 1, it was ready. White colonnaded palaces rose from 633 acres of lagoons, courts, plazas, islets and promenades. The whole admiring world gazed on both the tinsel and the purity of the "Great White City."

Six months the fair ran, and then it closed. The cloud-capped towers and gorgeous palaces came down. Winter winds returned to Chicago. And there, in the great city that had put up the wondrous fair, something like 100,000 jobless men shivered on street corners, slept in hallways, stood in long, ragged lines for an occasional bowl of charity soup. The World's Fair had opened at the same time as the most shattering depression in 20 years. Like the great Centennial show of 1876, also held during a time of economic distress, the Chicago spectacle called attention, almost mockingly, to the aching, mysterious gulf between 19th Century progress and poverty.

On President Grover Cleveland's broad shoulders fell a large share of the burden and the anguish of the depression. Cleveland must have felt at times that he was a star-crossed politician. In 1888 he had polled 5,537,857 votes to Benjamin Harrison's 5,447,129, but he failed to hold the White House when the peculiar workings of the electoral system wiped out his vote advantage.

COURAGEOUS IN CRISIS, Grover Cleveland was a strong president but a poor administrator. He was so loath to delegate authority that he hampered his staff in its work.

Cleveland swallowed his frustration, waited four years and secured his third Democratic nomination.

In 1892 he received almost 400,000 more popular votes than Harrison, as well as a safe lead of 132 electoral votes. Then, 10 days before Cleveland was to be inaugurated, the important Philadelphia and Reading Railroad went bankrupt. A wave of panic selling swept the stock exchange. The band music of inauguration day was more or less drowned out by the noise of the roof falling in. Before 1893 had ended, 500 banks had gone down, 16,000 business houses had closed and a full-scale economic crisis wracked the country. Cleveland had picked the wrong time to win.

It was now his fate to preside over four trouble-seared years. Hard times turned into fiery issues such facts as the dwindling availability of free lands in the West, the rise in the volume of immigration, the continuing consolidation of smaller business units into larger ones. Political parties groaned and wallowed like ships in a typhoon; prophets cried aloud from the housetops that America had gone after strange gods and was doomed; farmer, worker and businessman stirred and roared. The stage was being set for climactic events which would bring 20th Century America into being. The '90s would know birth and growth and what went with them—pain, pride of newness and yearning for the irretrievable passing day.

Thomas B. Reed, Speaker of the House during the "Billion Dollar Congress," was notorious for rounding up delinquent congressmen. Reed, pictured above as a bulldog, would scent out absentees and herd them to their seats. In an indirect acknowledgment that this technique lacked decorum, Reed barked: "A statesman is a successful politician who is dead."

THE decade had opened promisingly enough. The Republican 51st Congress had a busy legislative year in 1890. It passed the Sherman Antitrust Act and provided public largess for new classes of Civil War veterans (including those who had served as few as 90 days). The McKinley Tariff raised import duties to new plateaus.

Another measure, the Sherman Silver Purchase Act, committed the government to buying 4.5 million ounces of silver bullion monthly. The 51st managed to spend nearly a billion dollars, a then-incredible sum. When this was pointed out to the Republican Speaker of the House, Thomas B. Reed, he allegedly replied in good humor: "This is a billion-dollar country."

But the billion-dollar country was restless. Farmers, workers, and enemies of the railroads and the trusts were unimpressed with the 1890 record, and that autumn they elected a Democratic House. Two years later, it was made clear that the anger of the farmers ran deep.

During the '70s and '80s, there had been sporadic organization of farmers in the hard-hit wheat and cotton belts. By 1890, two large, loose groupings had appeared, known widely as the Northwestern Alliance and the Southern Alliance. Both Alliances had taken fliers in politics by endorsing candidates, and in a few states they were moving to capture the older parties. In South Carolina, for example, Alliancemen captured the 1890 Democratic state convention and nominated as governor (the equivalent to election in that state) Benjamin R. Tillman, a one-eyed, Negro-hating crusader for the dirt farmer. By 1892 the Alliances had decided that only a third national party would give them the fullest airing for their problems.

That party was born at a convention in Omaha in 1892. Hundreds of Alliancemen, along with Grangers, Greenbackers, Knights of Labor, prohibitionists and other reformers of every stripe, gathered to give national scope to the existing People's party (better known as the Populists). A veteran third-party candidate, James B. Weaver of Iowa, was nominated for the presidency; his platform demanded among other things the free coinage of silver at a ratio to gold of 16 to 1, direct election of senators, public ownership of rail, telephone and telegraph lines, and a graduated income tax.

Most significantly, the delegates cheered wildly at the reading of a preamble to that platform which declared that the nation was on "the verge of moral, political, and material ruin," that corruption dominated the ballot box and the bench, that labor was impoverished and "degenerating into European conditions," and that governmental injustice was breeding two great classes —tramps and millionaires. The fact that some Americans who for years had been placidly voting the Republican or Democratic tickets could roar approval of such an indictment of life in America was evidence that, even in the "prosperity" year of 1892, upheavals were in the making. In June, steelworkers in the Carnegie-owned plant at Homestead, Pennsylvania, went on strike. Henry Clay Frick, Carnegie's union-busting partner, promptly hired 300 private policemen of Pinkerton's National Detective Agency, which specialized in such assignments, to guard the locked plant.

Before the summer was over, there had been battles in which both Pinkertons and strikers had bled and died. The Populists had cried out that "a hireling standing army, unrecognized by our laws, is established to shoot [workmen] down." After a long contest the union was thoroughly defeated. Some 1,300 additional strikes marked 1892 as a year of stirrings.

Wheat prices averaged 62 cents a bushel, cotton was around eight cents a pound and corn 39 cents a bushel—prices close to or below the cost of production. A record 230 people—161 of them blacks—were lynched in 1892, the 30th year after the Emancipation Proclamation.

Such violence was not merely incidental. It was a sign of pent-up frustration, blindly seeking an outlet. Characteristically, Cleveland ignored this turbulence when he took his second oath of office—though the Populists in 1892 had won a million popular and 22 electoral votes, three governorships, five Senate seats, and many state and local offices.

In his inaugural address, Cleveland declared that the tariff should be reduced, that the "waste of public money" was a crime, that he would resist spoils and maintain "a sound and stable currency." It was a speech worthy of Thomas Jefferson—and in attempting to turn it into a legislative program, Cleveland very nearly made it the epitaph of the Democratic party.

An ingenious campaign badge of 1892 (above) shows the "Presidential Chair" and asks, "Who shall occupy it?" When triggered, the seat flips open and reveals a picture of Benjamin Harrison (below). Republicans wore such clever trinkets, but the campaign lacked verve since Harrison, grieved by the death of his wife, refused to make appearances. He lost the election.

CHEAP and honest government was simply not enough. As the depression tightened its grip in the opening months of 1893, the President's only response was to call the newly chosen Congress into special session in August and demand that it repeal the Sherman Silver Purchase Act of 1890.

Although Cleveland made a logical case, logic did not begin to comprehend the impact of the currency question. At the root of the matter lay complex, still-debatable questions of economics. But the debates over money in the United States in the late 19th Century were far more than technical discussions. They grew out of the deepening cleavage between sections and classes.

During the Civil War the government had pumped nearly $450 million of Treasury notes into the currency of the country. Later, when it attempted to retire these notes and resume specie payments, there were fierce objections. Many insisted that the growth in the nation's population and business justified an enlarged currency.

This argument was the source of the greenback agitation of the '70s and early '80s that enlisted small businessmen, angry over banks' refusals to grant loans. Even more attracted were Far Western farmers who had taken out mortgages when wheat was selling at two dollars a bushel, as in 1867, and who had to pay them off when wheat had dropped to 77 cents or less, as in 1878.

Meanwhile, there was the matter of silver. From 1792 onward, the United States Treasury issued both gold and silver coins. Beginning in 1834, silver was fixed at a value 1/16th that of gold. From 1834 until 1873, as it happened, the world prices of silver actually were a bit higher than this Treasury ratio suggested. Therefore silver bullion had a ready commercial sale and even coinage was melted for resale. Reflecting this, Congress in 1873 simply failed to provide for the further coinage of silver dollars. But within a few years huge quantities of silver began to pour out of Western mines, driving the metal's price to a point well below the old 16-to-1 ratio. The silver producers, bereft of markets, howled.

By 1880 preliminary moves were being taken for a curious marriage between millionaire mineowners and mortgage-bowed sodbusters. Greenbackers, also thwarted time and again in efforts to enlarge the currency by paper, allied themselves with the silverites. So bimetallism became the new cry of the inflationists. If the government took all the silver brought to it and coined it at 16 to 1, the amount of money in circulation would be increased, prices would go up, the yoke of debt would be less galling and there would be a sure market at fixed prices for silver. The proposal made political sense, too, since it would lure votes in the mining states.

Bimetallists railed against the law that had closed the door on silver coinage as part of a plot by the bankers and bondholders to increase the value of gold in plutocrats' vaults and drive down the prices received by the honest husbandman. In short, it was a crime—the "Crime of '73."

A political cartoon of 1889 titled "The Horn of Plenty" pictures James Tanner, the commissioner of pensions, recklessly flinging money to Northern veterans of the Civil War. Corporal Tanner expressed his fiscal policy in the remark: "I am for 'the old flag and an appropriation' for every old comrade who needs it." Such generosity quickly depleted the Treasury surplus.

BUT the bimetallists had no monopoly on hot passions. Defenders of the gold standard were equally vehement. They cried that if the United States could say that a quantity of silver 16 times as great as the quantity of gold in a gold dollar was *worth* a gold dollar, when commercially it was worth around 60 cents, then the government was legalizing the robbery of any creditor who lent a gold dollar and got back a silver one. The silverites retorted that it was robbery to lend a dollar worth one bushel of wheat and insist on being repaid with a dollar that bought two. To which the advocates of the gold-standard could reply that if the United States alone adopted bimetallism, international payment mechanisms would be hopelessly snarled, American credit abroad seriously compromised, and business and banking thrown into still further turmoil. Civilized countries of the world, said the conservatives, were on gold; the insane schemes of ignorant farmers and crackpot theorists could never change the inexorable laws of supply and demand; only anarchists and worse would propose to debase the currency and plunder honest and prudent investors for the benefit of failures and deadbeats.

By 1893 the discussion had passed beyond such academic issues as whether the purchasing power or the intrinsic value of currency was more important. The silverites were convinced that they faced a conspiracy of the "haves," with roots in Wall Street, in the Bank of England, in private European banking families like the Rothschilds and in every place where wealth meant power. The crusade for silver became a war against the trusts, the plutocrats, the bankers, the industrial East or whatever symbol of privilege a downtrodden group chose to hate at a particular moment.

On the other side stood the gold men, convinced they were defending property, tradition and the unchangeable laws of evolution and economics against a horde of wild-eyed fanatics. The "battle of the standards" became the carrier for emotions that had long been boiling, and for every man on either side who dimly understood the economic issues involved, there were scores to shout, march and fight under slogans that had little real meaning for them. It was a war of idols of silver and gold—an appropriate Armageddon for a generation reared on the Bible.

INTO this caldron Cleveland tossed his demand for repeal of the Sherman Silver Purchase Act. Under the act, the government was paying for silver in certificates that could be redeemed in either silver or gold. To Cleveland the choice was illusory. If the government did not pay its obligations in gold, faith in its solvency would be shaken and chaos would take over.

Therefore, the Treasury *had* to honor those certificates with payments of gold. But in effect this meant that the government was paying out gold to buy silver. This reduced the gold reserve, caused concern over the government's ability to pay its obligations and threatened to bring about all the grim consequences of paying in silver in the first place. Thus the government had to maintain the gold standard to keep the panic in check, but the Silver Purchase Act was draining an already reduced gold supply at a furious rate.

The necessity for repeal of the Silver Purchase Act was unmistakable to Cleveland. To get congressional approval was another matter. The Democrats controlled both houses, but this meant little, for the silverite schism ran through both parties. Nevertheless, if Cleveland used his powers to hold enough Democrats in line, he could win. His personal influence was indispensable and gold men shuddered at the thought of anything happening to him, since the Vice President, Adlai E. Stevenson, was a silver man.

To forestall such fears, there occurred an almost incredible episode in American history. In June of 1893, doctors discovered a cancer in the presidential mouth. Cleveland quietly boarded a friend's yacht. There he had a major operation which removed a large portion of his upper jaw and palate. The country remained in total ignorance, the bankers stood firm and by the first week in August the President, discreetly fitted with an artificial jawbone, was in Washington leading the fight for repeal. Two months later the press told the story, but it was indignantly denied. Since Cleveland was once again in booming, 200-pound-plus fettle with no scar showing, the denials were believed. Not until 1917 was the full story finally told.

After a long, hard fight, Congress repealed the Silver Purchase Act in October. Silver Democrats roared that they had been betrayed by Cleveland into the hands of the banking oligarchy. And repeal did not stop the drain on the Treasury's gold reserve, which sank and sank, far below the $100 million level considered safe. The Treasury had to float four bond issues from 1894 to 1896 to secure enough gold to avoid suspension of gold payments.

The third issue, in February of 1895, was bought and then resold by J. P. Morgan and by August Belmont, the American representative of the Rothschilds. The government realized about $65 million in gold and the bankers

Greedy industrialists, upholding the high tariffs, circle a steel colossus—"Our Infant Industry"—and carry placards which urge "protection and no competition for us." In the 1880s the opposition formed Free Trade Clubs and campaigned against the tariffs with slogans like "protectionism is the jugglery of the devil" and "a paternal government is an infernal government."

made an undisclosed profit. Although it was legal for Cleveland to turn to private bankers after public sale proved unsatisfactory, it was political suicide. Ever after, Cleveland was branded by soft-money men as the President who had gone groveling to the money masters to save the gold standard.

By 1894, however, Democrats were already aflame. Henry Adams noted that every congressional debate was "a four-sided fight; the republican attacks the democrat; the eastern democrat flies at the throat of the western democrat; all three then attack Cleveland." Governor Tillman of South Carolina bid for a Senate seat and earned his nickname of "Pitchfork Ben" by promising to "stick my pitchfork into [Cleveland's] old ribs" once he got to Washington. Missouri's Richard P. Bland—"Silver Dick" they called him—said that Democrats of East and West had "come to the parting of the ways" when Cleveland laid "the sacrificing hand upon silver."

In 1893, addressing a meeting, Congressman William Jennings Bryan declared that he would leave the Democrats if they adopted the gold standard and "serve his country and his God under some other name." The fact that he did not then do so was irrelevant. The wrath of a Tillman, a Bland, a Bryan, clearly showed that the silverites would soon make their bid, either to capture the Democratic party or desert it for Populism.

"Pitchfork Ben" Tillman, the South Carolina senator, was infamous for his bad manners, careless dress and hot temper. But his cursing brought him the most notoriety. Reproached by a missionary for using profanity, Tillman explained: "I assure you, my dear young lady, I made a careful comparison of the whole list of vices before I chose one for myself."

THE year 1894 saw things go from bad to worse to disastrous. There were two to three million unemployed, more than 12,000 business failures and almost a fifth of the nation's railroad mileage in receivership. It was a year, too, of strikes, of Coxey's Army, George Pullman, Eugene Debs, John P. Altgeld. And it was the year of publication for three stirring books whose pages still faintly echo an old anger—*A Traveller from Altruria, Wealth Against Commonwealth* and *Coin's Financial School.*

Jacob S. Coxey was nobody's failure. His quarrying and scrap-iron business in Massillon, Ohio, earned him a good income. Yet in him the idea burned that the government should solve the economic crisis through a unique inflation of the currency. Legal tender notes should be lent by Washington to local communities, which would pay them to unemployed workmen in return for labor on public works, roads in particular. The notion itself was not wholly lunatic, but Coxey had the zealot's vein of Quixotic unrealism. Who else would have named his son Legal Tender?

Accordingly, when Congress refused to legislate the Coxey plan, he announced that he would lead 100,000 jobless men—a "petition . . . with boots on"—to Washington to make a peaceful but irresistible demonstration. In March he left Massillon with approximately 100 men at his heels and a crowd of sardonic reporters who took delight in recounting the adventures of "General" Coxey and his mute, unarmed host.

As Coxey's men tramped along, their performance dwindled into comedy. The climax came when the "Army," 500 strong, reached the Capitol on the morning of April 29. On May 1 there was a scuffle with the police, some of the men were roughed up, and Coxey and Carl Browne, a religious charlatan who had joined the Army, were fined for walking on the grass. So ended social revolution in America. The country guffawed, but there was uneasiness too. Other armies of the jobless, some 17 of them altogether, had formed in California and elsewhere.

Few of them reached Washington, but everywhere America read about or witnessed firsthand a new spectacle—the shuffle of cold, hungry and shabby men living on handouts and hope as they begged their government to do something for them. Those who thought about it felt both pity and terror. The lone tramp was a minor annoyance or a joke, but an army of tramps?

And then, 10 days after Coxey's demonstration, the Pullman strike began. The cast that it brought on stage should have been assembled by a dramatist. First, there was George M. Pullman himself, a self-made inventor and contractor who had become a millionaire through the manufacture and leasing of his cars, in which men slept and dined their way across the country in mile-a-minute comfort. He was proud of his success, of his assembly shops in St. Louis, Elmira, Wilmington, Detroit, San Francisco and especially of his plant in Pullman, Illinois—a tract of land since absorbed into Chicago. There Pullman had created a model town named for him, free of the viciousness and dilapidation which blackened other company towns. Pullman's workers had an American standard of living—trim brick cottages, gaslights and running water, playgrounds, parks and churches.

But even utopia had to pay dividends. Pullman charged his workmen 20 to 25 per cent more than the going rent in neighboring towns. He resold Chicago water and gas at a proper markup and even had the town's sewage pumped to a company farm for fertilizer. Pullman thought his record enlightened by contrast with that of fellow employers, and it was. So he could scarcely have understood the resentment of one worker who noted: "We are born in a Pullman house, fed from the Pullman shop, taught in the Pullman school, catechized in the Pullman church, and when we die we shall be buried in the Pullman cemetery and go to the Pullman hell."

In the hard winter of 1893-1894, Pullman slashed wages—to save jobs, he insisted—without a corresponding reduction in rent. Most of the workers joined the new American Railway Union, which sent a delegation to ask Pullman to restore the cuts. Pullman refused. Whereupon the employees sullenly downed their tools and asked the national union for sympathy and support. That brought Eugene Victor Debs on stage.

Jacob S. Coxey (above) led his "army" of unemployed to Washington hoping to influence legislation. But his partner Carl Browne (below) had a messianic mission as well. Espousing an odd sort of reincarnation, Browne felt that he and Coxey represented the living parts of Christ's mind. Browne called Coxey the "Cerebrum of Christ" and named himself "Cerebellum."

DEBS, a mixture of Hoosier American and European revolutionary, was born in the packing town of Terre Haute, a year after his Alsatian father had settled there in 1854. He went to school until he was 14, quit and became a locomotive fireman, then threw all the energy of his tall frame into trying to carve out two or three careers at once. In 1880 he was simultaneously editor of the magazine put out by the Brotherhood of Locomotive Firemen, secretary and treasurer of the union and city clerk of Terre Haute.

Gradually, his instinctive sympathy and friendship for "working stiffs" made him a full-time union man. Later on in life, he would join the Socialists—five times he was their presidential candidate—and be remembered as a revolutionary in language but an easygoing, laughing disturber of the bourgeois peace. He was an idealist without self-righteousness; a Christian without a church; a "Red" who loved drinking bouts with his friend James Whitcomb Riley, the corn-fed Indiana bard; an "agitator" who retained the affection both of European-born socialists and of Midwestern Americans worlds removed from each other in language, tastes and feelings.

In 1894, however, Debs was not a Socialist, but a pioneer of industrial unionism on the railways. Only a year before, he had taken the lead in the

George M. Pullman perfected the sleeper coach; his Palace cars set a new standard in comfort and décor. In 1897 Robert Todd Lincoln became president of the Pullman Company. Years earlier the original Palace car, the "Pioneer," had been part of the train that took his father, the President, to his grave.

Adlai E. Stevenson, grandfather of the 1956 presidential candidate, was Cleveland's Vice President. Despite Cleveland's good intentions, the spoils system so swamped his Administration that Stevenson once protested a Treasury appointment only to realize later he himself had recommended the man.

creation of the American Railway Union. Membership was open to all white railroad men except managerial employees, for Debs believed that craft jealousies played into the hands of employers. The ARU got its baptism of fire in the early spring of 1894, when it won a strike on the Great Northern.

When the Pullman strikers asked for help in June, the ARU was in convention in Chicago. The ARU might have confined itself to sympathetic resolutions. Instead, Debs began by sending a committee to offer to arbitrate. But Pullman would not hear of it. On June 26 the ARU stopped handling Pullman equipment. The two dozen railroads serving Chicago refused to operate without Pullman cars. A major railroad strike followed. The Chicago roads, acting through the General Managers Association, had decided that the time was right to break the ARU. The lines were able to call upon powerful assistance in the form of the Attorney General of the United States, the third leading player in the unfolding drama.

Richard Olney was a rare bird—a wealthy Massachusetts corporation lawyer who habitually voted Democratic. He was also hot-tempered and stubborn, and wholly contemptuous of reformers, agrarians, labor leaders and other apostles of the unwashed. Ignoring the fact that as Attorney General he represented the workers too, he confided to a friend that the strike could be made "a failure everywhere" if management got an immediate injunction forbidding any attempt to interfere with the mails and interstate commerce. The granting of such an order would, he expected, create sufficient violence by the union to open the way for the introduction of federal troops.

The request was made, and the federal district court issued an injunction on July 2 that prohibited any interference with the operations of the railroads. Since it was impossible to conduct a railroad strike without so interfering—however peaceably—the injunction would have put an end to the ARU boycott of trains with Pullman equipment. Obedience to the order would also have destroyed the ARU. Debs decided to ignore the injunction.

There was mob violence in freight yards near Chicago, in a repetition of the scenes of 1877. A headline shrieked: "Strike Is Now War." Hastily, and before any real damage was done, Olney prevailed upon Cleveland to order federal troops into the city. It was then, and by almost all objective accounts not until then, that trouble really began. The troops were assisted by some 3,600 specially deputized marshals (actually chosen by the railroads), numbering a good many young hoodlums eager to break union heads. On the other side were thousands of the miserable vagrants of Chicago's preceding winter of discontent, ready for trouble.

BETWEEN July 5 and July 8, the situation exploded: Mobs surged into the yards and burned boxcars and buildings, fired shots, smashed windows; the worst fears of conservatives seemed on the verge of realization. But the strike was weakening. On July 10, Debs and other union leaders were arrested for obstructing the mails, released, and rearrested a week later. By then the strike was dying. There were many aftermaths—among them the ultimate collapse of the ARU (which did not displease the craft unions), the conversion of Debs to socialism while serving a six-month jail term for contempt of court and the beginning of a remarkable turn in the career of Clarence Darrow, a young Chicago lawyer who handled the union's case.

There was one other postlude. The blame for the violence was placed squarely on Olney and Cleveland by John Peter Altgeld, governor of the state of Illinois and himself a Democrat. Altgeld insisted that the situation had been entirely in control and that he himself, with a state militia, could have protected life and property without breaking the strike.

The German-born son of an immigrant, Altgeld was as incorruptible and as deeply set in his own grooves as Cleveland. As a young man Altgeld served in the Civil War, worked as a day laborer, painfully taught himself law, corrected his accented English and made the hard climb to success. He became a judge, a wealthy speculator in Chicago real estate, finally governor in 1892. But his spirit did not belong with his fellow businessmen and barristers. Viewing the men who stood in shabby bitterness before him in court, Altgeld worried intensely about the Americans who had fallen off the ladder of respectability or had never even reached the bottom rung. His first published work was a little treatise, *Our Penal Machinery and Its Victims.*

When the voters of Illinois sent him to Springfield, he was quickly confronted with a specific penal problem. Three of the Haymarket anarchists were still in jail. Altgeld, studying the trial record, decided that they had been victims of injustice and pardoned them. Despite protests that this would encourage anarchists to murder at will, Altgeld bluntly disdained compromise. He held firm—and wrecked his political career.

Although Eugene V. Debs was called a "king" during the Pullman strike, his union position did not save him from a prison term for contempt. Debs felt that the American system was biased and said: "The judicial nets are so adjusted as to catch the minnows and let the whales slip through . . ."

THE entire nation felt the shock of the Pullman strike. Conservatives were dismayed by the governor's sympathy for laboring men who had defied the courts. And for those who felt that the country was in the grip of plutocracy, the Pullman strike was almost a last straw. To them, the railroad owners merely had to snap their fingers to have judges and soldiers come rushing to force workingmen back to underpaid and unorganized labor. How much further, they wondered, could the degradation of Lincoln's America go?

Meanwhile, books of protest appeared, written by men who believed that America must be purged and reformed to be made fit anew for its mission. As early as 1879, Henry George, an ex-sailor, newspaperman and miner, had published *Progress and Poverty,* an inquiry into the "increase of want" that went everywhere in the modern world with the "increase of wealth" like some hideous Siamese twin. George blamed private ownership of land for all the world's troubles. Land, the source of all natural wealth, George said, increased in value as civilization advanced. Since the increase went into the pocket of the landlord, labor and capital were deprived of needed economic nourishment. Land monopoly was the mother of all monopoly. The solution was the "single tax." Let government tax this unearned increase in land value and want could be ended.

Nine years after the publication of George's book, Edward Bellamy wrote a utopian novel, *Looking Backward.* In it a young Bostonian of 1887 fell into a trance and awoke in the year 2000 to find himself living in a co-operative, up-to-date paradise, without panics, strikes, millionaires or paupers. This was accomplished, it was explained to him, by carrying the trust movement to its logical conclusion. The nation had become "the one capitalist in the place of all other capitalists, the sole employer, the final monopoly . . . in the profits and economies of which all citizens shared." So enchanting did Bellamy make his profit-purged Eden that hundreds of Nationalist Clubs were formed, enlisting thousands of Americans who would accept socialism in this palatable form. Both George's single-taxers and Bellamy's Nationalists furnished votes to the Populists from 1892 on.

In 1894 the sound of dissent became even more audible. William Dean Howells published *A Traveller from Altruria*. A gentle book, it was kindled by Howells' interest in Christian Socialism, as expounded by Leo Tolstoy, the Russian novelist, and by various English and American thinkers. It is the story of a visitor from the mythical Altruria who is shown American life for the first time, after having studied America's ideals through its literature. Everywhere he finds betrayal of the professed values. Selfishness, exploitation and snobbism are deplored in theory and defended in practice by the social and intellectual leaders whom he meets in a summer hotel.

What made *A Traveller from Altruria* important was its very lack of stridency. Howells, a genial and popular American novelist, moved in the best drawing rooms and had believed "the more smiling aspects of life" to be the most characteristically American. Criticism from a Howells in soft tones was harder for some to bear than the condemnations of a Populist.

In another book, *Wealth Against Commonwealth*, by a Chicago editor, Henry Demarest Lloyd, the tone was one of harsh denunciation. Lloyd did not spare the whip from his opening observation, "Nature is rich; but everywhere man, the heir of nature, is poor," to his closing appeal to "the body of the commonalty" to throw off the yoke of predatory wealth. He blasted trusts in general, and Standard Oil in particular.

Still another social document of 1894 was *Coin's Financial School*, the work of W. H. Harvey. "Professor Coin," a fictional finance expert, presented lessons in a catechism form. "The money lenders," he told his pupils, ". . . have a selfish interest in maintaining the gold standard. . . . They believe that if the gold standard can survive for a few years longer, the people will get used . . . to their poverty—and quietly submit."

Three hundred thousand copies of *Coin's Financial School* with its simple answers were sold within a year. Yet even books which affected more complex economic arguments, like *Progress and Poverty*, were stamped with the hallmark of American thought in that innocent, though unhappy, age—the assumption that a single remedy would automatically restart the parade of progress. But this generation of reformers, unlike earlier dissidents, was likely to look to the government—federal, state or local—for remedial action.

It was no longer enough to roar at the monster Bank, as in Jackson's day, and assume that virtue would triumph once the enemy was crushed. Now, it seemed, men would have to act through political agencies in positive ways before individualism could win. There was still a hopeful feeling that rescue was in sight, if society would only *do* something. That faith in action linked the Nationalists, single-taxers, Populists and even certain American socialists firmly to the optimistic American tradition.

"Will somebody show Uncle Sam how to see through the silver trouble?" asks this cartoon, which ridicules the government's currency policy. Uncle Sam, with coins for eyes, pleads: "I am silver blind. Please assist me." The assistance, however, was slow in coming, and the economic controversy over silver grew into a major political issue which cut across party lines.

WHEN all was said and done, the problem was: do what? One thing the American voter in a depression could do—he could turn out the party in power. The black year of 1894 came to its end with the elections of November, and when the ballots were counted the Democrats had suffered stunning blows—more stunning than they realized. They lost both houses of Congress and would not regain either of them for 16 long years. What was more, the Populists had increased their vote by 42 per cent over 1892, elected four senators, four representatives, 21 state executive officials, 150 state senators and 315 state representatives. Many other successful candidates, running as Republicans or Democrats, had strong Populist leanings.

The brush fire of reform was spreading and the Supreme Court fanned the flames. The newly formed Interstate Commerce Commission had been finding it impossible to win decisions against the railroads in the federal courts. In effect, the Interstate Commerce Act was being nullified. Now, a test arose of the government's power and will in the matter of monopolies. In 1895 the Supreme Court considered the case of *U.S. vs. E. C. Knight Co.* The company involved was the American Sugar Refining Company, a combination which controlled (according to some estimates) 98 per cent of the manufacture of refined sugar in the United States.

WITH involved logic, the majority of the justices decided that the company involved was engaged only in the *manufacture* of sugar, which, nestled within a state boundary, was protected from federal intervention. The United States might use its authority only to interfere with the restraint of trade in *commerce*. To the nonlegal mind, the message was clear: Monopoly or near-monopoly in the manufacture of any article would not be condemned under the Sherman Act. The trusts were safe for a while. A few rejoiced. One was Attorney General Richard Olney, who had in his own words "taken the responsibility of not prosecuting under a law I believed to be no good. . . ."

Four months later, in May, the court spoke again. The preceding summer had seen passage of the Wilson-Gorman tariff bill which did little to lighten duties, but which contained one sop to the reformers in the shape of a 2 per cent tax on incomes of $4,000 or more. The new levy was promptly challenged, and in *Pollock vs. Farmers' Loan and Trust Co.* the justices heard arguments designed to prove that the income tax was an assault upon property. A majority agreed that the measure was unconstitutional because it was a "direct" tax that could be levied only in proportion to population.

As one dissenting justice—Kentucky's fierce, outspoken John Marshall Harlan—put it, the effect of the decision was "to give to certain kinds of property a position of favoritism . . . and to invest them with power and influence that may be perilous to . . . the American people. . . ."

The next week the court upheld the injunction against Debs in the Pullman strike. So, as the third winter of the depression approached, there was ground for belief that the Supreme Court, like the President and the Congress, was conspiring with the rich against the poor. With corn down to a quarter a bushel, wheat 50 cents, cotton less than eight cents a pound and with the jobless still clustering before boarded-up shops and factories, passions were high.

Old men remembered that things had been much like this 35 years before. Then, too, there had been a third party rising—Republican rather than Populist. Then men had cursed the Slave Power instead of Wall Street. A Democratic President had fought with his own party, and the Supreme Court's name had become a hissing and a reproach, for a decision that bore the name of Dred Scott, instead of E. C. Knight. And after all that, there had come the collapse of everything, the falling of the heavens, the ultimate catastrophe of Civil War. What form would the new apocalypse take? As the presidential year of 1896 opened, a tense people waited to find out.

Populist leaders cling to what their enemies considered a "platform of lunacy." A patchwork of interests holds the party balloon together—Knights of Labor are placed beside Grangers and Greenbackers. Although conservatives derided the Populists, farmers sang: "The railroads and old party bosses together did sweetly agree" to deceive "hayseeds like me."

SHODDY MATERIALS used for the fair's construction inspire a caustic lampoon. Like the plaster hand in the dismayed grasp of a sightseer, the fair was not built to last.

Coming-of-age party in Chicago

THE gleaming statues and stately exhibition palaces were flimsy—a birthday-cake icing of plaster daubed on temporary frames. But the illusion they created was striking. Visitors from all over America and from distant corners of the world flocked to the Chicago World's Columbian Exposition in 1893. They came away with a kaleidoscopic reminder of the past (the fair celebrated the 400 years since Columbus discovered America) and a vision of a new age of power and enlightenment. There were gigantic dynamos churning out electricity, man's new white magic; soaring domes and miles of Grecian columns. Fiercely mustachioed gondoliers, brought to Chicago from Venice, sculled awe-struck passengers on a network of canals. An old man summed it all up to his wife: "Well, it paid even if it did take all the burial money."

More than 27 million people paid 50 cents apiece to enjoy everything from a five-million-dollar art exhibition to the gyrations of a bevy of exotic dancers. What made the fair important, though, was not its financial success but the lesson that it offered: The United States had come of age faster than it knew. Before the fair, Chicago was considered a provincial city, a pale imitation of an Eastern metropolis. Afterwards no one could deny that it was a center of culture on its own. Astute observers from abroad saw in the impressive exhibits in science and industry the portent of America's international greatness.

A COLORFUL POSTER for the fair's commemoration of 1871 Chicago fire shows the Manufactures Building (and the 275-foot dome of the Administration Buildi

OLD WORLD INFLUENCE is visible in a painting of the fair's South Canal. It includes *(from the left)* an Egyptian obelisk, Machinery Hall with twin spires in Spanish Renaissance style and, at far right, a neoclassic palace devoted to electricity.

NEW WORLD DESIGN is seen in Louis Sullivan's sharply original Transportation Building, relegated to a back lot because it clashed with the fair's white façades. But the functional excellence of the structure earned it a special French award.

Facades, fishes and
a shelter for the fair sex

THE heart of the fair *(left)* looked like a stately blend of Rome, Paris and Atlantic City. The ornate Old World architecture was to have a lasting influence on the lines of American public buildings, but it outraged the budding school of functional architects. Unsophisticated Americans, however, reveled in the miniature world tour the fair provided. What other chance would most visitors have to see a reproduction of a doorway from Bordeaux's cathedral? One notable sign of change was the Woman's Building. Offering cooking lessons and a model nursery, it was at first downgraded by the fair's planners, then belatedly praised for treating woman as "part of the body politic, instead of a . . . social integer."

FULL-SCALE AQUARIA in the Fisheries exhibit drew visitors who could watch anything from sharks to "plebeian catfish," then, perhaps, retire to an adjacent "fish restaurant" for dinner.

Dedicated to the Managers of Cairo Street

World's Columbian Exposition 1893

Cairo Street Waltz

1893
8 F38 M1
6 m. 193

LITH BY THE ORCUTT CO. CHICAGO

PRICE 50 CENTS

EXOTIC RHYTHMS of the fair's Middle Eastern dancers are evoked in this popular song named after the area where they performed. Visitors, lured in with cries of "Come, handsome infidel strangers," were treated to abdominal gyrations by heavily draped girls. The performance was called a *danse du ventre*, for "belly dance" sounded naughtier in a foreign tongue.

SHREWD ADVERTISING in the *Youth's Companion* magazine stresses the need for comfortable shoes to get around the fair's 633 acres.

LOFTIEST VIEWS of the fair heighten the appeal of the 250-foot wheel designed by G. W. Ferris to rival the 1889 Paris Exposition's Eiffel Tower. Each glass cab held 60 passengers. Several couples tried vainly to get married in the top car.

HIGHEST LINE OF VISION, 258 feet.
HIGHEST POINT OF WHEEL, 264 feet.
DIAMETER OF WHEEL, (center of pins) 250 feet.
TOTAL WEIGHT OF WHEEL AND CARS, 2100 tons.
TOTAL WEIGHT OF PEOPLE PER TRIP, only 150 tons.
AXLE STEEL FORGED—largest ever made—33 inches diameter and 45½ feet long, weighing, with spiders attached, 70½ tons.
TIME REQUIRED FOR ONE TRIP, 20 minutes.
DUPLICATE REVERSING ENGINES, 1000 horse power each.
TOTAL WEIGHT of wheel, levers and machinery, 4300 tons.
CARRYING CAPACITY, 36 CARS, all being 31 feet, 9 CH feet 6½ in.

Far-flung pleasures of the midway

THE two things no visitor could miss—however shod or propelled (*right*)—were a spin on the world's first Ferris wheel and a peek at the sinful byways of Cairo Street. Both were located at some distance from the other exhibits, on the Midway Plaisance, a strip largely devoted to what one observer grandiosely named "the ethnological congress"—encampments of strange peoples from all over. A group of "cannibals" from Dahomey in West Africa did not eat in public, but obligingly posed looking smug and full of memories. Soon the air was alive with ethnic observations. Cairo Street dancing girls, it was bruited about among fairgoers, were "homely as owls" but had "voluptuous feet." Candy made in the Algerian and Tunisian Village "looked like wool and was nearly as palatable." Happily, ethnic influence worked both ways. In no time at all the Dahomans were plaintively asking for "Chicago beer," a phrase which, no doubt, had its uses even for a cannibal.

CHAIR-MEN'S CHORES are the subject of a humorous cartoon showing an overstuffed patron viewing the sights. Rolling chairs, usually with one pusher, were rented for 75 cents an hour.

99

A brilliant glow of hope

White as frosting, immense as the turreted palace of some mythical potentate, the Electricity Building glowed with the light of thousands of bulbs and sent shimmering images to haunt the dark waters of the canals. For visitors, whose cities were still lighted by gas, whose villages and isolated homes

knew only oil lamps or candles, the building's fascination was practical as well as esthetic. Inside, the first working electrical locomotive was on display. A man could watch as invisible electric power carved glass and plated base metal with gold. He could gaze in wonder at Edison's kinetograph, a device which "transmits scenes to the eye as well as sounds to the ear." The Electricity Building manifested the widespread and exhilarating faith that man was becoming endowed with miraculous knowledge. As yet undimmed by wars, the new century was just around the corner, limitless and entirely hopeful.

CROWN OF THORNS
USED
BY BRYAN.
IN CAMPAIGN SPEECHES.

SPEECH TORN FROM THE BIBLE

FROM THE BIBLE

USED IN BRYAN'S
CHICAGO SPEECH
CROSS OF GOLD.

SPEECH PLAGIARIZED FROM THE BIBLE

BIBLE

ANARCH

HAMILTON

5. A CLAMOROUS AND FRENZIED CAMPAIGN

ALL his life, the poet Vachel Lindsay remembered that as a boy going on 17 in the city of Springfield, Illinois, in 1896, he had seen wonders and heard prophecies. For at a rally, there was revealed to him William Jennings Bryan, a man who was more than a man—who was the voice of the West, the new, the untrammeled, the heavenward-gazing America that had been Lincoln's and must not be McKinley's. Bryan was ... well, Bryan was:

> Candidate for president who sketched a silver Zion,
> The one American Poet who could sing outdoors . . .
> In a coat like a deacon, in a black Stetson hat
> He scourged the elephant plutocrats
> With barbed wire from the Platte

Although Bryan was captivating the imaginations of countless small-town boys with torchlight parades and speeches through the countryside, less favorable views of his candidacy would find wide expression. The New York *Tribune*, for example, called the architect of the silver Zion "a puppet in the blood-imbued hands of Altgeld, the anarchist, and Debs, the revolutionist. ... He had less provocation than Benedict Arnold, less intellectual force than Aaron Burr, less manliness and courage than Jefferson Davis. He was the rival of them all in deliberate wickedness and treason to the Republic."

That was the tone of presidential politics, 1896 vintage. Looking back, the

WILLIAM JENNINGS BRYAN is pilloried *(opposite)* as "The Sacrilegious Candidate"—a reference to his Cross of Gold speech that electrified the 1896 Democratic convention.

passions that broke men's hearts or terrified their spirits in that campaign seem old-fashioned. Yet there were real issues at stake and real powers to be won. Amid the tumult two national political parties were being hammered into the shape they would present for the first 30 years of the 20th Century.

Three sets of political managers scanned the barometers of opinion in the spring of 1896. There were the usual Republicans and Democrats. There were also the Populists, an important factor after their upsurge in 1894.

The Republicans had alternated, lean years and fat, with the Democrats. The White House changed hands in 1884, 1888 and 1892. Within the Republican party there remained a basic cleavage between the idealism that attended the party's birth and the high-stepping opportunism of the Grant era —but the line was blurring. The tariff, however, remained a cherished article of faith to the Republicans. In any case, tariff sponsorship was not a Republican monopoly. Grover Cleveland could not get any real tariff reduction through the Democratic-controlled Congress in 1894.

As for the civil service issue, Republican independents could still complain about spoilsmanship, but the dirty business was conducted with less of the brazen, broad-daylight arrogance that men like Zach Chandler had displayed in the '70s. Finally, the party bosses no longer waved the bloody shirt: it had lost its appeal.

Although Union veterans were still important, they were now outnumbered by younger voters. The prairie farmer, supposed beneficiary of the 1860 Republican planks barring slavery from the West and advocating the Homestead Law, was no longer uniformly loyal. His gratitude had dwindled with his hopes of wealth. He listened intently while the Populist told him that Republicanism had suckled his enemies: the monopolists who controlled railroads, money and grain-elevator rates and the price of barbed wire, twine binders and jute bags. The Republican party had to win loyalties in new areas and among new classes to survive beyond its 40th year.

Grimly important, William Mc-Kinley is paired with Garret Hobart, his running mate, on this 1896 campaign umbrella. McKinley was linked with "Protection." Hobart was saddled with "Sound Money." Republican delegations went to McKinley's home in Canton, Ohio, preceding the election, bringing gifts. The most annoying present was five American eagles.

BUT the challenge was also an opportunity, if the Republicans could come up with a candidate and an issue that united all the old factions and once more made the party look truly national and forward-looking. The times were kind to them. In June the shrewdest political strategist in years gave them their candidate. In July the Democrats handed them their issue.

The political mastermind was Marcus Alonzo Hanna. The candidate was William McKinley. Both came from Ohio, a state neatly suspended between a frontier past and an industrial future—a perfect political laboratory in which manufacturing and agriculture, factory town and country village, native and foreigner, old New England and old Virginia descendants rubbed elbows. Aside from this common Ohio birth, McKinley and Hanna seemed to have little in common. But both represented complementary parts of the Midwestern American character. They needed and liked each other.

Hanna, born in 1837, grew up in Cleveland, where his father had a grocery business, and numbered among his boyhood acquaintances young John D. Rockefeller. After his marriage to the daughter of a successful coal and iron merchant, Hanna became a prosperous businessman. By the time he was 50, he owned a large coal and iron business, part of Cleveland's street railway system, a newspaper and various other properties. He was likable but blunt and forthright, a generous employer who did not make the slightest effort to disguise his paternalism. On the other hand, he was a conservative businessman who refused to mouth the platitudes of social Darwinism. Both qualities were admirably illustrated in his reaction to George Pullman's refusal to arbitrate with the workers in his company town. Said Hanna: "A man who won't meet his men half-way is a God damn fool."

Having made his fortune, Hanna yearned for the fresh excitement a political career might offer. He held as an article of faith that American prosperity was best assured by an alliance between politics and business. To him, the best illustration of the possibilities in such a match was the growth of American industry behind a Republican-built protective tariff.

Yet Hanna himself was not the stuff of which candidates are made. He was meant to do best as the manager for others more persuasive with the public at large, and for such a task he had formidable powers of organization and fund raising among his business contacts. After early efforts for several aspiring Ohio politicians, he met his perfect subject, William McKinley, who was, in Hanna's eyes, the very model of a Republican, a gentleman, a patriot and a Christian.

Mark Hanna (above) in a hostile cartoon (below) is a statue watching his banker friends remove the deposed figure of Washington. Similarly, the New York "Journal" relentlessly identified Hanna with greed and corruption. Of McKinley's alleged submission to Hanna the "Journal" warned, "Hanna and the others will shuffle him and deal him like a pack of cards."

M CKINLEY was a small-town lawyer from Canton, Ohio. In the Civil War he rose in rank from private to major in the 23rd Ohio, commanded by Rutherford B. Hayes, who became a close friend. Aiming at a public career, McKinley got to Congress in 1876 and remained in the House with only one two-year lapse until 1891. He made a reputation as a student of the tariff and a defender of maximum protection; the 1890 tariff bore his name.

Otherwise he had not committed himself politically. McKinley was so enamored of America's industrial growth that he simply could not perceive how such growth might pose problems for the simple, democratic order in which he grew up. He did not dodge issues. Often he merely did not see them.

Besides, McKinley was a man of great sweetness and personal attractiveness. He had a high forehead, handsomely broad chest and shoulders (though the years finally gave him a prominent belly), and was an almost incredibly devoted husband to his wife, a neurotically dependent invalid. He was a nondrinker (except for an occasional glass of wine in later life), an abhorrer of profanity and off-color stories, a Methodist regular in church attendance. He could talk self-confidently about purity, nobility and ideals, to the eminent satisfaction of both the respectable ladies and their storekeeping husbands who ruled small-town America.

In 12 years in Congress as a faithful Republican, McKinley had unquestionably learned when to look the other way and when to be conveniently absent-minded. Yet he retained the aura of personal incorruptibility. Hanna, according to one authority, was "drawn to McKinley's scruples and idealistic standards, like a hardened man of the world who becomes infatuated with virgin innocence." Certainly McKinley admired Hanna's achievements. "Together," it has been noted, "these two made one perfect politician."

After backing McKinley in successful bids for the Ohio governorship in 1891 and 1893, Hanna retired from his business responsibilities in 1895 to give full time to McKinley's candidacy for the 1896 Republican nomination. Hanna was a good host with an ample purse; to his home in Cleveland and to a winter residence thoughtfully chosen in the South came a stream of party luminaries. Hanna wined them, dined them, cigared them and extolled the merits of his good friend. When the convention gathered in St. Louis in June, McKinley won an easy first-ballot nomination.

The only question really open was the party's attitude on money. McKinley, embarrassed by his congressional record of bimetallism, ambiguously urged maintenance of "the present standard." But a strong group supported a more specific declaration in favor of gold. The platform finally called for preserving "the existing gold standard" as that of "the most enlightened nations of the earth." Hanna let the gold men think McKinley had yielded up his bimetallism as a favor to them, and thus made new friends in the party.

In point of fact, bimetallism was coyly toyed with in the platform statement that the Republicans opposed free coinage of silver "except by international agreement with the leading commercial nations of the world, which we pledge ourselves to promote." (But that was overlooked as soon as convenient.) The move toward gold cost the Republicans some silver-state adherents, who formed a splinter "Silver Republican" party, but in the long run it was a vast advantage. In June, however, they could not know this.

Shortly after his nomination, McKinley told a friend that he was strictly a tariff man on a tariff platform. "The money question," he said, "is unduly prominent. In 30 days you won't hear anything about it." "In 30 days," was the answer, "you won't hear of anything else." It was a statement of both truth and value to the Republican cause. The Democrats were to make money the central issue and lose on it. Yet for a few hot July days the political heirs of Jackson erupted in excitement and hope.

PARTY conventions seldom ignore their own incumbent Presidents, but in 1896 Grover Cleveland's policies were repudiated. The platform adopted in Chicago on July 9 condemned "the trafficking with banking syndicates," "arbitrary interference by federal authorities in local affairs" and "government by injunction"—clear rebukes to the President for his bond-selling agreement with Morgan and his handling of the Pullman strike. The platform showed Altgeld's influence; with the convention in his back yard, he intended to keep it out of the hands of the Eastern hard-money Democrats.

He had plenty of help from such anti-Cleveland party members as "Pitchfork Ben" Tillman as well as from Western silverites. Silver men were clearly in the saddle, and the real fighting, if any, would be over the nominee. As the Republicans had gathered with an almost certain candidate and no clear issue, so the Democrats seemed to have an issue and no candidate. Altgeld was ineligible by virtue of foreign birth. No Western or Southern Democrat seemed in a commanding position. Since 1868 the Democratic party had run four candidates from New York and one from Pennsylvania. Rural Democrats were determined to break this North Atlantic domination.

The question of the standard-bearer was answered dramatically in the debate over the platform. The silver men had inserted a declaration in favor of "the free and unlimited coinage of both silver and gold at the present legal ratio of 16 to one. . . ." The outnumbered gold Democrats on the Resolutions Committee submitted a minority report favoring both the gold standard and the Cleveland Administration. Speeches were scheduled for both sides. Bryan, the youthful but well-known champion of the silver men, closed their arguments. He stood up before the 20,000 perspiring people packed into Chicago's old Coliseum, drew a deep breath, confidently opened his thin, wide mouth

Richard Parks ("Silver Dick") Bland spent years prospecting in California and practicing law in the Ozarks. Although his experience made him a lucid congressman for miners and farmers, he lacked the passion needed to fire the imagination of the Free Silverites. This failing lost him the presidential nomination to the messianic William Jennings Bryan.

and prepared to launch himself into history and legend on a golden voice.

Bryan had lived for this moment. He was born in 1860, the son of Silas Bryan, a lawyer, judge and state legislator of Salem, Illinois. From his father he inherited a taste for politics, and from both parents a strong religious drive which was directed into the revivalistic activities of the period. Bryan believed that the Lord God Jehovah had made the cosmos and left a literal record of that creation—plus direction for the future management of His handiwork— in the King James Bible. God had also made the common people; whatever a majority of them desired was clearly His will; what that majority believed was His truth. Raised in a Democratic family and region, Bryan fervently believed that the party of Andrew Jackson embodied that truth—especially in its old hostility to monopolies, banks and tariffs, its espousals of agrarian virtue, small business and free competition. On these abiding principles he founded his faith and his ambitions.

As a boy he had first aspired to be a preacher, then played at being a senator. After attending little Illinois College, he studied law. Then he merged both his boyhood dreams. He would build a political career on his ability to win audiences. To improve his prospects, Bryan moved out to the growing prairie town of Lincoln, Nebraska. At 30 he was just what William McKinley had been at the same age—a young attorney graduated from a fresh-water college to a small-town practice and faithful to the party of his elders.

But McKinley's town was Canton, in the northeastern corner of Ohio, where cities like Cleveland, Akron and Youngstown had already shifted to an industrial pattern and learned to live with the machine age. Bryan began his political climbing in the heart of the Great Plains wheat belt, an area seared by hard times and far from the centers of power. Thus, circumstances made Bryan—in most respects as orthodox as McKinley—a rebel. He learned that in Nebraska the voice of the people was a voice of discontent, and that a Democrat should heed it if he did not wish to lose out to Populism.

Bryan became a silver man on the simplest of grounds. "The people of Nebraska are for free silver," he explained once, "and I am for free silver. I will look up the arguments later." He adopted this point of view after he was elected to Congress. But when he won a second term, in part by embracing the silverite viewpoint, he delivered a sensationally eloquent speech against repeal of the Sherman Silver Purchase Act, and thus found a crusade.

BRYAN would fuse his evangelical outlook, Democratic inheritance and personal strivings into a unique amalgam. He would lead the battle to drive the money-changers from the temple of the republic. When it was won, the meek—that is, the downtrodden rural hosts—would inherit the earth. Unfortunately Bryan was hindered in his evangelism by an inconvenient circumstance. In 1894 he failed to win a Senate seat, partly through the opposition of the Democratic boss of Nebraska, a Cleveland supporter. To keep his name and his message in print, the "boy orator of the Platte" then became editor of the Omaha *World-Herald,* financed by silver miners. In the crowded convention hall in Chicago, he at last had the national press waiting and listening.

It is easy to discount Bryan as a man whose horizons were constricted, whose intellect was shallow, who was wholly out of touch with the scientific and industrial developments shaping the modern world. But this underestimates his influence in the '90s. The symbols that his rich voice manipulated

John Peter Altgeld (above), though wary of Bryan's ability, went along with his party and backed Bryan's quest for the White House. Conservatives called Altgeld "a slimy demagogue" and a ruthless Catiline eager to repudiate the national debt. In the cartoon below he is accused of hiding his anarchistic firebrand behind the innocent mask of Bryan and Free Silver.

107

still had deep emotional significance for a nation just then reluctantly abandoning some—but not all—of the old moralities and verities. (It remains a source of both strength and confusion that Americans have never entirely separated politics and morals.)

What was more, Bryan voiced protests that ran both wide and deep, that had some foundation in justice. In Chicago, he was, for millions, an old-fashioned conscience, boldly rebuking America for the idols it had come to worship.

He struck the note quickly: "The humblest citizen in all the land, when clad in the armor of a righteous cause, is stronger than all the hosts of error." Then the well-rehearsed Biblical phrases were marshaled into order. The silver Democrats, he declaimed, "went forth from victory unto victory until they are now assembled, not to discuss, not to debate, but to enter up the judgment already rendered by the plain people of this country."

Around those plain people Bryan threw the mantle of social respectability. Did the gold men complain that the silverites were threatening the business interests of the country? "We say to you that you have made the definition of a business man too limited in its application. The man who is employed for wages is as much a business man as his employer; the attorney in a country town is as much a business man as the corporation counsel in a great metropolis; the merchant at the crossroads store is as much a business man as the merchant of New York." The small-town delegates were leaning forward now, and the buzzing of voices had died down. The palm-leaf fans were stopped in mid-swing. And, "bidding the eagles of the West fly on," as Vachel Lindsay put it, Bryan continued: "We have petitioned, and our petitions have been scorned; we have entreated, and our entreaties have been disregarded; we have begged, and they have mocked when our calamity came. We beg no longer; we entreat no more; we petition no more. We defy them!"

And with defiance thundering, the heroes of the republic and the party—Jackson and Jefferson—were marched forth. Bryan evoked the Jeffersonian ideal of the yeoman supporting the nation on his shoulders. "You come to us and tell us that the great cities are in favor of the gold standard," rang out the mighty voice. "Burn down your cities and leave our farms, and your cities will spring up again as if by magic; but destroy our farms and the grass will grow in the streets of every city in the country."

William A. Peffer, the Populist senator from Kansas, was famous for his long beard and vague thinking. He gave speeches on finance which were tedious and full of statistics, and wrote books on farm reform which were self-contradictory. In his muddled way he was dedicated to Free Silver, and argued his views with a fervor that was "intense, narrow, and fanatical."

THE tension was palpable in every seat and aisle. The climax came in words used before by Bryan; they would offend some with a hint of blasphemy. But neither of those things mattered. It was not a moment for prudence, novelty or even logic. A century of evangelical stirring, of westward movement, of democratic striving was eloquently shouting its defiance and its valedictory: "Having behind us the producing masses of this nation and the world, supported by the commercial interests, the laboring interests and the toilers everywhere, we will answer their demand for a gold standard by saying to them: You shall not press down upon the brow of labor this crown of thorns, you shall not crucify mankind upon a cross of gold."

There was dead silence as Bryan walked to his seat, then a shout, then bedlam—a mad demonstration that choked the aisles and rocked the rafters. In the excitement people forgot that the silver men had all the votes they needed to win the platform fight. Though the "cross of gold" speech was magnificent, it only stampeded the convention in the direction it was moving.

Yet in another sense the speech and the nomination were vastly significant. They keyed the whole campaign to Bryan's personality and outlook. His youth, his fundamentalism, his lack of readiness to debate any issue but the silver question seriously—all left their mark. No wonder that Altgeld—an urbanite and a foreigner and therefore immune to Bryanism—declared that "it takes more than speeches to win real victories." He lamented Bryan's failure to face up to the varied tensions which stemmed from the rising industrial, urbanized society. Bryan was still speaking for a simpler America, a point underscored shortly after the Democratic nomination, when the Populists also made him their nominee. They did not do so without a battle. Some of the People's party founders regarded that nomination as a coming-of-age. Others thought it suicide.

HISTORY has not been invariably kind or discerning in dealing with the Populist movement. It is still under the shadow of many accusations leveled against it in the '90s. It has been called a crusade of cranks and fanatics, a mysterious outburst of unlikely rural radicalism, the farmer's last squirming as the "toils" of finance capitalism clamped around him—even an uprising of Midwesterners against a fancied conspiracy of bankers, Easterners, Englishmen and Jews, a kind of precursor of Fascist isolationism. It is not easy to weigh such charges. For the party had emerged as an independent organization in 1892 and died, for all practical purposes, after 1896—too short a time to assume a clearly defined character.

Moreover, in those election years Populists in various states joined with others from the two older parties in efforts to unseat the dominant "ins." In Republican strongholds like Kansas, Populists worked with Democrats to support fusion candidates for a wide variety of offices. In the South the Populists often clasped hands with whatever was left of Republicanism, and men became governors, sheriffs and assessors as the joint nominees of both "minority" parties against the entrenched Democrats. Sometimes Populists tried to capture the Democratic machine. Hence, there is almost no "pure" Populist vote to analyze.

Yet some things can and should be said. The Populists *did* have in their ranks a number of well-publicized eccentrics (or alleged eccentrics)—men like Kansas Congressman Jerry Simpson, who had been a single-taxer and a Greenbacker before swinging to Populism. Once, in a debate with a Republican, Simpson alleged that his snobbish rival was the kind who wore silk socks. A reporter, noting Simpson's homespun appearance, wrote that Jerry probably wore no socks at all, and the nickname "Sockless Jerry," with its oddball connotations, pursued Simpson for the rest of his life.

Another Populist worthy was plump and pie-faced Ignatius Donnelly of Minnesota, a gifted talker and a pre-eminent champion of panaceas. The Populists also presented Senator William Peffer, a serious-minded farm spokesman whose long beard made him look like the newspaper caricature of a yokel. And there was Mary Elizabeth Lease—the "Kansas pythoness"—a hottongued Irishwoman in her thirties who studied law after bearing four children and who urged farmers to raise "less corn and more *Hell*."

Yet thousands of Populist workers and officials were as sane, to say the least, as their Republican and Democratic neighbors. The Populists were no

A "Patrick Henry in petticoats," Mary E. Lease spoke widely and wildly for the Populists. When she toured the South, one local newspaper hotly declared: "Southern manhood revolts at the idea of degrading womanhood to the level of politics." From statements like this, Bertrand Russell reasoned that Victorian men put their women on pedestals to keep them powerless.

more eccentric as a group than many Southern Democratic demagogues. Even the most easily derided Populists—Simpson, Donnelly and Peffer—had attracted no attention when they had been Republicans.

Nor was Populist "radicalism" composed of moonbeams and fanaticism. In 1892 the Populists favored a government-managed currency, a graduated income tax, postal savings banks, the direct election of senators and government ownership of railroads and telegraphs. All but the last proposition were to become law before long without overturning the foundations of society—and all had been proposed and discussed for years by minority parties. These ideas might have been shocking to some, but not for their novelty.

Populism was not even an uncomplicated revolt of the agrarian against the victorious urban world. In 1894 the states which gave more than 30 per cent of their votes to Populists and fusionists were only 12 in number: Montana and Washington and Colorado, where silver sentiment was more important than any farmers' discontents; South Dakota, Nebraska, Kansas, Texas, Louisiana, Alabama, Georgia and both Carolinas. In such states as Wisconsin, Iowa, Missouri, Illinois and Indiana, where farming was still very important, Populism and fusion won less than 15 per cent of the ballots.

The dairy farmer, the vegetable grower, the corn and hog raiser resisted the call of Populism. The new party did best in the hard-hit wheat and cotton belts. Populism was not simply a movement of farmers who lamented the declining importance of rural America; it was an "uprising" of farmers who were at the end of their rope after years of drought, chinch bugs, crop liens, interest charges and, above all, declining prices.

In an acid comment on Bryan, a trusting workingman stoops with a coin balanced on his neck while the Democratic candidate wields the sword of "wild-eyed finance" and says: "I propose to cut your dollar in two without hurting you a particle." One Republican virtuously pledged his loyalty to "a dollar that can stand up and say, 'I know my Redeemer liveth.'"

WHAT mattered in 1896 was not the reality of Populism as much as the kind of anxieties it nourished among conservatives. Populism's evangelistic zeal kindled memories of abolitionism. Its bold demands for federal intervention in the economy stirred fears of an assault on property—the small holders against the large. If the Populists put their seal of approval on Bryan, all the terrors conjured up by the "revolutionary" program of the People's party would attach themselves to him.

When the Populists gathered in St. Louis, it was clear that a sizable faction had decided that Bryan's nomination made sense. A separate Populist ticket could not win and might help McKinley in a few key states. But a Populist-Democrat combination might well succeed. The Populists would then at least have free silver and a President from the prairie farm belt who might, in time, even smile kindly on the rest of the Populist platform. In any case, it was a half loaf or none.

This viewpoint was resisted fiercely by go-it-alone Populists (or "middle-of-the-road" men, as they called themselves). As Georgia's Tom Watson put it, the Democratic idea of fusion was that "we play Jonah while they play whale." And Henry Demarest Lloyd, sensing that the Bryan of 1896 was, for all his rhetoric, a conservative who would ignore every Populist demand except the one for silver, opined that "the Free Silver movement is a fake."

Nevertheless the union with the Democrats was consummated. The People's party married itself to Bryan and free silver. This went down hardest with the Southerners who had been hounded and harried in their home states by the Democrats they were now asked to embrace. The Southerners were most vociferous in claiming that the party had destroyed itself. Time seemed to bear them out, since Populism never was a serious contender after 1896, though it lingered on as a wraith until 1908.

But in a larger sense the union with the Democrats made Populism a national phenomenon, forcing its attitudes and grievances into public attention from seaboard to seaboard, no matter what Bryan did or did not say. Within a few years after 1896, Populism's principles of strenuous national action to equalize opportunity and control the ambitions of organized wealth would no longer belong to the political underground. They would be debated by major candidates everywhere. In good, evangelical fashion the party had died in the prospect of a glorious resurrection.

This cartoon ridicules what many voters believed—that William Mc-Kinley, once elected, would wave a wand and usher in an age of plenty. Certainly the great financiers who backed the Republican "sound dollar" program believed in the magic of his political powers. When they heard of his election they cavorted like children and wound up "dancing in each other's arms."

ALL this was far from clear as the campaign got under way in July. The only certainties were the vigor of Bryan and the horror of the orthodox. The very day after the Democrats adopted their platform at Chicago, a Philadelphia editor shrieked: "No large political movement in America has ever before spawned such hideous and repulsive vipers." Then he went on: "This riotous platform is the concrete creed of the mob . . . intensified and edged with hate and venom. It rests upon the four corner stones of organized Repudiation, deliberate Confiscation, chartered Communism, and enthroned Anarchy." In London the elegant Republican John Hay wondered if the "Baby Demosthenes" would, upon election, abolish the Supreme Court, confiscate the railroads and make Eugene Debs Attorney General.

The vigorous president of New York City's Police Commission, Theodore Roosevelt, was quoted as having said: "I speak with the greatest soberness when I say that the sentiment now animating a large proportion of our people can only be suppressed, as the Commune in Paris was suppressed, by taking ten or a dozen of their leaders out, standing them against a wall, and shooting them dead." Roosevelt denied the words later, but they were in character. In Emporia, Kansas, the youthful Republican editor of the town's *Gazette*, William Allen White, wrote an editorial titled "What's the Matter with Kansas" in which he asserted that Populism's aim was to "put the lazy, greasy fizzle who can't pay his debts, on an altar, and bow down and worship him." But both Roosevelt and White were later to change their minds and make reputations advocating Populist-inspired reforms.

On the other side, Bryanites did their best to depict McKinley as the tool of the trusts and the puppet of plutocrat Mark Hanna. Much was made of the fact that Hanna had led a syndicate which bailed McKinley out of $130,000 worth of debt during the depression. In the big cities Democratic precinct workers hustled voters to registration booths, serenely unconcerned with such trivial matters as either the identity of the nominee or the platform.

And there was the tireless effort of Bryan himself, traveling 18,000 miles in 21 states, speaking five and six times a day, proclaiming the farmer's message throughout the land on a campaign fund of some $250,000 contributed mainly by silver magnates. It was an inspiring spectacle, but shrewd Mark Hanna sensed presently that Bryan was undoing himself with his endless repetition of the "cross of gold" motif. "He's talking silver all the time," said Hanna, "and that's where we've got him."

For McKinley's mastermind realized that the entire American business world—Democrats included—was genuinely frightened by the prospect of inflation, the flight of gold into hiding, the collapse of banks and of insurance companies, disaster. Counting on this nervousness, Hanna proceeded to levy campaign-fund assessments on business companies throughout the nation.

The fund he built, estimated at between $3.5 million and $10 million, was used to flood the country with pamphlets, cartoons, posters and buttons, to organize parades and demonstrations and to bring delegations from every segment of the population to Canton. McKinley remained at home. Benignly he received his visitors on the front porch, listened to the speeches on which he had been well briefed and replied with carefully planned "extemporaneous" oratory defending the tariff, sound money and the Grand Old Party.

Under this barrage the American voter became convinced that the only issue of the campaign was "honest money." Urban workers were told—and they believed—that their wages would be turned into worthless tinsel if the Democrats triumphed. There were other means of persuasion. Many factory owners were alleged to have told their hands on election eve that if Bryan won, there was no point in returning to work Wednesday morning.

Amid tumult and shouting, then, the campaign moved to decision. When the ballots were counted, amid a tension as great as had prevailed in 1860 or 1876, Hanna's triumph was impressive—even though 6.5 million voters had gone for Bryan as against slightly over 7 million for McKinley. But Bryan had won only the Solid South and the Mountain States, plus Washington, South Dakota, Nebraska, Kansas and Missouri. All of these states were marked by either relative poverty or a thin population. The Republicans, on the other hand, had captured everything north of the Ohio river and east of the Mis-

1894: HIGH-WATER MARK OF POPULISM

This map shows by state the percentage of votes cast for Populist candidates in the election of 1894, when their cause reached its peak of 1.5 million votes. Clearly Populism was strongest in the West Central and Southern states. Here dissident farmers and small traders, whose grievances were aggravated by severe depression, voted Populist to defend their interests against the rising power of industry and banking. But after the 1894 election Populism dwindled as its adherents, discouraged by the failure of minority protest, returned to the two major parties.

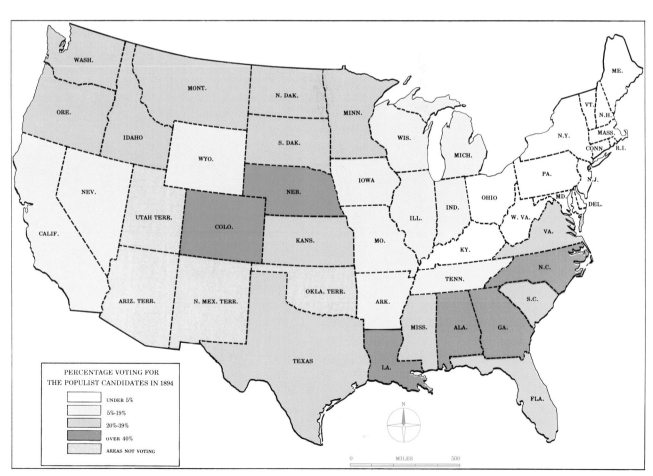

PERCENTAGE VOTING FOR
THE POPULIST CANDIDATES IN 1894

UNDER 5%
5%–19%
20%–39%
OVER 40%
AREAS NOT VOTING

souri, with Kentucky and West Virginia, Oregon and California for a bonus.

It was in that northeast quarter of the United States, however, that they had won—in New England, New York, Pennsylvania, Ohio, Illinois. In the states where mill and refinery puffed smoke, where rivers were greasy with factory waste and farmers loaded their wagons in the dawn hours for the trip to the city produce market—that was where the strength and the power lay, against which the Democrats and Populists had been broken.

For 1896 made all this Republican territory. Bryan lost because the urban worker did not turn out for him. The urban worker had his grudge against the factory, but knew that his wages depended on keeping it running—and after the 1893 crash, he trusted the Republicans to do that job better. Bryan lost because the Michigan and Indiana and Illinois farmer voted against him. That farmer had sentimental yearnings for the pioneer days of "agricultural supremacy," but he also knew that with his kerosene lamp and his mail-order overalls he was better off than his grandfather who burned pine knots and wore deerskin. The farmer might curse Standard Oil and the tariff for raising the price of his kerosene and overalls, but he trusted McKinley and Hanna to provide them, as he feared that Bryan would not.

Bryan lost, finally, because he had identified himself with yesterday. The West and the South might follow him, for a time at least, but they were not enough. The Republicans, on the other hand, had not only enlisted the big battalions, but they had made a successful change of base. No longer were they the party of the Union and free soil. They were now the party of industry and prosperity. In small-town chambers of commerce, for the ensuing 30 years and more, the venerated portraits of Republican Presidents would beam down from the walls like saints at a feast of financial plenty.

The city, the factory and that part of the agricultural world closely tied to the city and the factory voted for tomorrow—and tomorrow won. The Republicans would control the federal government—House, Senate and Executive Mansion—until 1911, and then lose only through an intraparty split.

Yet if there was rejoicing in the headquarters of the trusts, it was premature. The conservative victory was not complete. Within the Republican party itself, an old, idealistic leaven was at work, passed down from Free-Soilers to Mugwumps to a new breed that would come to call itself "Progressives." Many Populists were reabsorbed into both the old parties. Neither their lessons nor the fright they had caused were forgotten. Before long, Republican Presidents would move against the trusts, the railroads, the despoilers of public lands, the practitioners of fraud against consumers. And when a Democratic President took office in 1913, he would propose and carry out a program of reforms.

THE nation, in short, had not given an unrestricted mandate to the masters of capital. It had only signified its political acceptance of the machine age. The voters did not yet quite see the problems of the approaching 20th Century—of how to contain great aggregations of power within the democratic framework, neatly balancing liberty, plenty and order. What they had said with their ballots was that the nation could survive depression without a dismantling of the modern world. Still reeling from hard times but with slowly re-awakening confidence, they faced the future under McKinley. Within a little more than a year after his inauguration they were to learn that tomorrow contained a surprise—not only prosperity, but empire.

Home-loving William McKinley is seen on the front porch from which he conducted his campaign. His mother wanted him to be a clergyman and she never quite reconciled herself to her son's political career. On the morning of the inauguration the President-elect's brother attempted to convince the determined old woman that the high office was "better than a bishopric."

A SMALL TRIUMPH from Twain's *Adventures of Tom Sawyer* shows Tom *(left)* at his memorable fence-painting chore, tricking another lad into doing the job. Along with most of Mark's books, this classic of boyhood was highly autobiographical.

A WORLDWIDE SUCCESS, Mark Twain *(opposite)* takes his ease on shipboard during his globe-girdling lecture tour in 1895. Twain, who said "I moralize well," was fond of signing his pictures with wry epigrams like the one at the bottom.

The adventures of a native son

IN the 1870s, while East Coast intellectuals argued over new sciences and new heresies, ordinary Americans were laughing their way through the prolific output of a new writer from the West. He was Samuel Langhorne Clemens and he wrote under the pen name Mark Twain. He called humor "the good-natured side of any truth," and this definition is exemplified in his self-description: "Born 1835; 5 feet 8½ inches tall; weight about 145 pounds . . . dark brown hair and red moustache, full face with very high ears and light gray beautiful beaming eyes and a damned good moral character."

Twain's phenomenal success was built on the soundest of foundations. For like Mark himself, his writing was "the very marrow of Americanism." His readers were right at home with his colloquial joshing, his stubborn individualism, his passionate republicanism. They had his nostalgia for youth, his love for the land, his affection for people and human foibles, his restlessness and ambition. They wanted to see through his eyes the picaresque life these qualities had brought him: his adventuresome boyhood, the likes of which were fast fading with the frontier; his foot-loose young manhood; his pilot's career in the halcyon time of Mississippi steamboating; his good times in the West's boisterous mining camps; his triumphant junkets to distant places which seemed all the more fascinating for his irreverent—and reliably American—attitude toward them. So his countrymen took this native son to their hearts, and they made Mark Twain an institution in his own lifetime.

Be good & you will be lonesome.

Mark Twain

THE BAREFOOT HERO of *The Adventures of Tom Sawyer* happily fishes in a first-edition sketch. Twain called the book "a hymn put into prose to give it a worldly air."

THE EARLIEST PICTURE of Sam Clemens shows him at 15, as a printer's apprentice on the hometown newspaper. His father's death forced him to work for food, lodging and the publisher's old clothes.

Storing up boyhood memory in a town by the river

SAM CLEMENS was four in 1839 when his family settled in Hannibal, Missouri (*below*), a young town thriving on small industry. To Sam as he grew up, the wonderful thing about Hannibal was the Mississippi. Over a thousand riverboats docked there each year, and he never tired of running to the landing on the cry of "Steamboat a-comin'!" He ranged far and wide on the awesome river and in the sweet woodlands, and in between he picked up another kind of education in school.

In 1848, to relieve his family's straitened finances, Sam was apprenticed to the publisher of the local *Missouri Courier*. "I became a printer," he later wrote, "and began to add one link after another to the chain which was to lead me into the literary profession."

By the time Sam was 18 he had a trade, a yen to make an easy fortune, a need to see the world. So he ran away from "the white town drowsing in the sunshine." But his 14 years in Hannibal had enriched him with an overpowering love for his youth, and in his books and in his memories he kept returning there all his life.

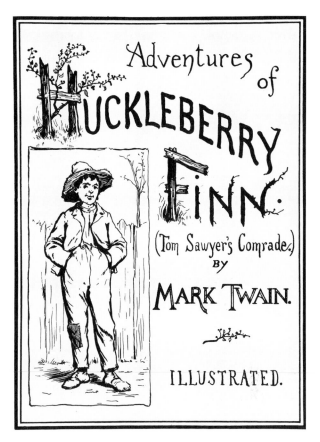

A QUAINT COVER announced *Huckleberry Finn*, widely considered Twain's greatest book. Huck was modeled after a forbidden friend of Sam Clemens' youth, Tom Blankenship.

THE PIRATE CREW, comprised of Tom Sawyer, Huck Finn and Joe Harper, goes voyaging on their first captured vessel. Young Sam Clemens himself was no less an expert at purloining boats and stealing watermelons.

SAM CLEMENS' HANNIBAL, on the Mississippi beyond Lover's Leap (*far left*), beckons a northbound keelboat. Sam was often hauled from the water "in a substantially drown[ed] condition."

PILOT Samuel Clemens *(left)* sports whiskers about 1860. As a pilot he often heard the boatmen yell "Mark twain," meaning that the water was 12 feet deep. Later, seeking a pen name, he chose the term.

A PILOTHOUSE, typical of those Clemens used, boasts a stove, the wheel and a clear view to all sides. Often this "sumptuous temple" was located amidships on the top deck, as on the boat below.

Belching smoke, the triple-decked "Mississippi" gets up a full head of steam. Like this gallant old stern-wheeler, former pilot Sam Clemens

A prideful career as a Mississippi riverboat pilot

IN 1857, tramp printer Sam Clemens left his job in Cincinnati to pursue a get-rich-quick scheme in South America. But his plans changed suddenly as he boarded a southbound steamboat. His boyhood yearning to be a river pilot returned with an irresistible rush.

"I planned a siege against my pilot," he later wrote, "and at the end of three hard days he surrendered. He agreed to teach me the Mississippi River from New Orleans to St. Louis for $500, payable out of my first wages after graduation." Slowly Sam mastered the 1,200 miles of tricky currents, cutoffs and sand bars. In April 1859 he "graduated" and received his pilot's license.

For two years, until the Civil War ended his career, Sam enjoyed life aboard the floating palaces, but enjoyed his work even more. He said: "The face of the water, in time, became a wonderful book . . . which told its mind to me without reserve. . . . It was not a book to be read once and thrown aside, for it had a new story to tell every day." Years later he sadly wrote, "I loved the profession far better than any I have followed since."

outlived the river's romantic heyday. Sam said of steamboating as it steadily declined, "A strangely short life for so magnificent a creature."

This mountain boom town is Virginia City as Twain found it in 1862. Half of its inhabitants "swarmed the streets like bees and the other

IN THE MODE, Twain at left is dressed like a miner as he writes in Virginia City, while at right he wears a neat outfit— perhaps for his trips to cover the legislature in Carson City.

Twain out West: "I am wild with impatience to move!"

RESTLESS, Sam Clemens went west in 1861 with his older brother Orion, who had been named secretary of the Nevada Territory. Sam drifted off, into the exciting world of the silver camps. He dabbled at mining and newspaper writing until Virginia City's *Territorial Enterprise* offered him $25 a week as a full-time hand.

It was in Virginia City *(above)* that Sam Clemens grew into his pen name and became Mark Twain. His rough companions sharpened his writer's eye and ear. His joshing articles on local crimes and high jinks soon began appearing in Eastern papers. Later, still ruled by whim, he landed a real reporting job in San Francisco, scratched for gold in Angel's Camp, and set out for the Sandwich Islands. "All I know or feel," he wrote, "is that I am wild with impatience to move—move—*move!*"

half swarmed among the drifts" of the silver mines directly beneath.

LOSING CONTROL of his bargain horse, Twain *(above)* attains "unexpected elevation" in an illustration from *Roughing It*. This book of his Western adventures found many eager buyers. His fractious nag, however, he had to give away.

LOSING A CONTEST, the victimized frog in Twain's "The Celebrated Jumping Frog of Calaveras County" squats with its belly full of bird shot as its rival *(right)* makes the winning leap. The short story established Twain as a top humorist.

121

The author as lecturer and New England squire

A BICYCLING KNIGHT is one of the sketches Twain ordered for *A Connecticut Yankee in King Arthur's Court*. He began the book in 1866, but interruptions delayed its publication until 1889.

PARALYZED with fright, Mark Twain faced his first lecture audience in 1866 in San Francisco. His New York debut next year was a qualified success: "People were positively ill for days, laughing at that lecture," but most of them had been admitted free. Then in 1868, after a Mediterranean trip that produced his book *The Innocents Abroad* and gave him a new lecture subject, he set out in earnest to make his talks pay. He also met and courted Olivia Langdon of Elmira, New York.

Love and lecturing triumphed together. Mounting acclaim for Mark's droll performances wore down the opposition of Livy's proper parents, who considered his dress and manners quite alarming. Mark and Livy were married in 1870. By 1874 they were happily set up in the comfortable Hartford house in which they would live for 17 years. Here, with his family *(below)* growing up around him, Twain poured forth his greatest books.

A SHREWD STYLIST on the lecture platform, Twain *(opposite)* slyly eyes his appreciative audience. He "most cordially" hated lecturing but returned to it in 1895 to pay off business debts.

A CONTENTED FAMILY surrounds Twain on the porch of their Hartford home in 1885. Between the author and his wife Olivia sits Jean, five. Clara, 11, is at left and Susy, 13, at the right.

"I am seventy . . . and would take my rest"

"I CAME in with Halley's Comet in 1835," said Twain, "and I expect to go out with it." He did, when the comet next appeared in 1910. The last decade of Mark's life was a sorrowful one: his wife Livy died in 1904 and his daughter Jean in 1909. But it also brought him financial security and many honors *(below)*. For his 70th birthday he was given a testimonial dinner at Delmonico's. Nearly 200 prominent writers attended, and they wept unashamedly at Mark's moving speech. He concluded: "I am seventy; seventy and would nestle in the chimney corner, and smoke my pipe, and read my book, and take my rest, wishing you well in all affection. . . ."

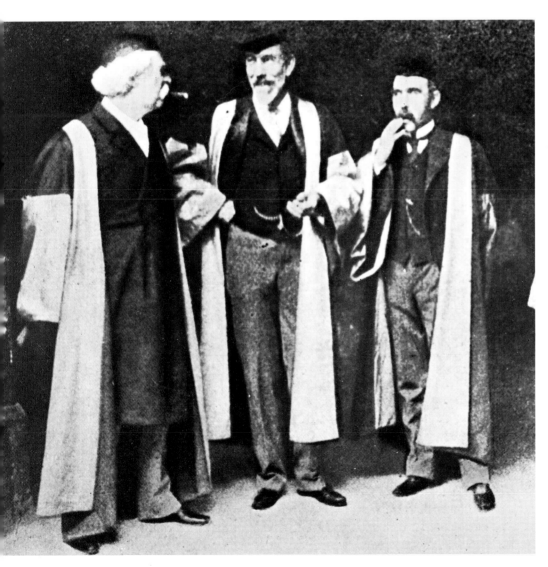

RECEIVING AN HONORARY DEGREE at Oxford, Twain *(left)* renews acquaintances with Rudyard Kipling *(right)* in 1907. As they left the ceremony, Mark was surrounded by a huge cheering crowd which escorted him to the college gates.

There do seem to be so many diffi....

....and just put my whole heart in it....

......and there's so many other privileges, that... perhaps....

Oh, never mind, I reckon I'm good enough just as I am.

TWAIN'S MOODS in the pictures at left and above inspired his whimsical explanation: "This series . . . registers with scientific precision, stage by stage, the progress of a moral purpose through the mind of the human race's Oldest Friend."

6. THE "SPLENDID LITTLE WAR"

WILLIAM MCKINLEY was a good-tempered and optimistic man, and his inaugural address on March 4, 1897, breathed serenity and hope. Business was still shaky, but "prompt, energetic and intelligent action" by Congress could do much to improve it. Despite four years of depression and the angry 1896 campaign, America's "precious free institutions" were as beloved as ever; the new President even sensed a "fraternal spirit . . . and . . . manifestations of good will everywhere." Looking to further horizons, the ex-major made it clear that the same brotherliness would guide America in its foreign relations. "War should never be entered upon until every agency of peace has failed," he declared. "Peace is preferable to war in almost every contingency. Arbitration is the true method of settlement of international as well as local or individual differences." Ironically, the following year he would sign a declaration of war against Spain and be the first wartime President in 33 years.

Henry Adams, as pessimistic as McKinley was hopeful, observed in a letter: "Slowly and painfully our people are waking up to the new world they are to live in. . . ." Adams was understating the situation. For, with innocent enthusiasm and fluttering ideals—not "slowly and painfully"—the American people, under McKinley, were rushing into the rips and undertows of world politics. Adams could see that the coming war would "throw open an immense new field of difficulties." He simply had no idea of the capacity of

WATCHING THE ACTION, Commodore George Dewey directs the battle of Manila Bay from his flagship. Dewey rose from anonymity to fame after this awesome victory.

his countrymen for believing that their wealth and righteousness could overcome difficulties.

Even before the Civil War, there had been some American interest in possible expansion southward to absorb the rest of Mexico and all of Central America. After the battle flags of the Union and Confederate armies had been furled, interest in expansion picked up again. It was Grant, the hero of Appomattox, who in 1869 heard the future calling seductively from warm semitropic waters. As President he received overtures from the dictator of Santo Domingo (now the Dominican Republic) indicating that the little nation would not object to annexation by the United States. To Grant, this seemed an admirable notion. As he put it, if Santo Domingo became American, "the soil would soon have fallen into the hands of the United States capitalists," who were friends and heroes of the old soldier. An annexation treaty, prepared at the instigation of some American speculators, was proposed but the Senate rejected it.

Elsewhere, a 10-year-long insurrection against Spanish rule had begun in Cuba in 1868. Despite an incident in 1873, when the Spaniards captured a rebel-owned ship illegally flying the American flag and shot a number of its crewmen, including some Americans, the United States avoided war. A small indemnity payment by Spain settled the matter.

For over half a century, American whaling skippers and China traders had made the Stars and Stripes familiar in the Pacific. In 1854 Japan agreed to open trade with the United States. In 1867 an American naval officer took possession of a little-known atoll in mid-Pacific known as Midway. Alaska, which was purchased in 1867, was considered to be a frozen and remote storehouse of fish, furs and just possibly more valuable assets. In 1878 the United States, in full solemnity, signed a treaty with a "prince" of the Samoan Islands granting Americans a coaling station at Pago Pago. And in 1887 the King of Hawaii gave the United States a lease upon a fateful roadstead called Pearl Harbor. In making this agreement, King Kalakaua bowed to the resident American traders, sugar planters and missionaries who already dominated the islands.

Hawaii's Queen Liliuokalani, the composer of "Aloha Oe," was immoral, said malicious gossips, because she enjoyed watching hula dancers. But to expansionists, her worst misdeed was insisting that Hawaii be run by Hawaiians and remain free. Her stubborn resistance led to Yankee-inspired revolution, and the islands were annexed in any case—"for their own good."

BY 1890, then, the idea of the Stars and Stripes flying over consular offices and drydocks in far-off Pacific water had already been planted. Changing world conditions made it likely these seeds of empire would germinate quickly. For one thing, there was the revolution in sea war: Sailing vessels, with holds full of provisions, powder and shot, could cruise for months without touching land except, perhaps, for a quick stop at some islet to fill water casks. But steam-driven ironclads, though faster and deadlier, were more restricted in range. They needed depots of coal and spare parts, so places like Midway and Samoa were cherished by the American navy.

Moreover the '70s and '80s saw a steady march of European "protectors" into Asia and Africa. The flags of France, England and Germany floated over Burma, Indochina, Malaya, Rhodesia, Togoland, encouraging Americans to feel that a growing nation did not weigh in the balance of history if it confined its power to its boundaries. Were Americans shouldering their share of the white man's responsibilities?

At bottom this ferment was caused by social Darwinism, which tied history, science and national pride into one self-justifying package. In 1885 John

Fiske said that "the work which the English race began when it colonized North America is destined to go on until every land on the earth's surface that is not already the seat of an old civilization shall become English in its language, in its religion, in its political habits and traditions."

A Congregational clergyman, Josiah Strong, predicted in *Our Country*, published in 1885, that the Anglo-Saxon race "of unequaled energy, with all the majesty of numbers and the might of wealth behind it—the representative . . . of the largest liberty, the purest Christianity, the highest civilization . . . will spread itself over the earth."

I N 1890 a new voice was heard. It came from a 49-year-old naval captain, Alfred T. Mahan. Mahan's book, *The Influence of Sea Power Upon History*, became (along with his later writings) holy writ to a generation of big-navy spokesmen. (Kaiser Wilhelm II made Mahan's works available aboard German warships; Queen Victoria and the prime minister of England invited the captain to dinner when duty brought him that way.) Mahan argued that command of the seas—through possession of a great fleet, overseas bases, colonies and a merchant marine—guaranteed trade, wealth and security to a people and, thus, liberty and progress. The history of England, he said, was glorious proof of this proposition. Spain and France had declined through ignoring it. The American nation should ponder the lesson well.

Mahan had little reason to expect, in 1890, that the United States would heed him. America's foreign trade was on the increase; the value of its exports, only $281 million in 1865, would reach almost $1.4 billion by 1900: nearly a fivefold expansion. Imports in the same period rose from $239 million to $850 million. Yet at the end of the century, almost 85 per cent of this trade was carried in foreign-flag vessels. There was no great American merchant marine for a navy to protect. Later on it would be claimed that American overseas expansion was a case of the flag following the dollar; the facts of the 1890s make this claim a flight of fancy. Mahan was not urging his countrymen to defend an existing mercantile greatness, but to build a great navy, as befitted a giant power, and then make use of it.

The country did not appear to be listening in 1890. Yet Mahan's ideas, combined with those of men like Fiske and Strong, reflected the general chestiness of the nation, which sensed its industrial power. Mahan, Fiske and Strong had influence with an important intellectual, social and political group. America might not be imperially-minded yet, but it would be ready for the purple when greatness was thrust upon it. And between 1893 and 1898, the initial shoves of destiny came.

The first push came in Hawaii. In January of 1893 the white residents and landowners of the islands—mostly Americans—staged a revolt against Queen Liliuokalani to forestall the possibility that she might recapture the power that had passed to their hands. These men wanted something more than local control: They were hell-bent for annexation to the United States, which would restore the special trade advantage their sugar had formerly enjoyed in America.

The American minister to Hawaii, John L. Stevens, a dedicated annexationist, considerately ordered a landing party of some 150 armed men brought ashore in Honolulu from an American cruiser to provide protection for life and property—though neither appeared to be visibly threatened.

The son of a professor at West Point, Captain Alfred Thayer Mahan went to Annapolis, where he was described as "very good looking and the smartest man in his class." His guiding principles— that a nation's prosperity depended on its navy and that colonies were indispensable as "resting-places" for the fleet—were well received by imperialists everywhere.

Stevens immediately recognized the government set up by the rebels, and a treaty of annexation was drawn up and laid before the Senate.

Benjamin Harrison's Administration was in favor of this sort of "spirited" diplomacy, a policy particularly relished by James G. Blaine, the Secretary of State from 1889 to 1892. Blaine had already agreed, in 1889, to tightening the American grip on Samoa by participation in a protectorate over the islands along with Germany and Great Britain. The Hawaiian treaty, however, was still in the Senate when Grover Cleveland took over on March 4, 1893. Cleveland, who regarded an empire as an expensive and un-American luxury, pigeonholed the treaty. The newly created Republic of Hawaii had to wait until 1898 before it could once more hope to join the Union.

Cleveland's disapproval of Hawaiian annexation did not mean he would follow a pacific policy. In 1895 he and his Secretary of State—Richard Olney, the hot-tempered Attorney General of Pullman-strike fame—brought the country to the brink of war with Great Britain. The British were disputing the boundary of British Guiana with Venezuela. Cleveland and Olney, flaunting the Monroe Doctrine, insisted that Queen Victoria's government submit the question to arbitration.

The British were unimpressed and at first refused. Their navy mustered 32 battleships to five for the United States. But a war would have been inconvenient and expensive, would have exposed Canada to invasion and called the British forces away from more pressing work around the globe. So the British agreed to arbitrate the question, but in the meantime American jingoism was crackling. "This country needs a war," wrote Theodore Roosevelt to Henry Cabot Lodge in 1895, and added that only "bankers, brokers and anglomaniacs" favored "peace at any price."

Although these martial ambitions came to nothing in that year, Roosevelt's war was in the making. A fresh insurrection had broken out in Cuba. Before peace returned there, Theodore Roosevelt and some other Americans would have their taste of uniforms, glory and death.

T HE Cuban revolution was a thoroughly unpleasant one. The rebels, controlling the countryside, could not overcome the Spanish garrisons in head-on fighting, so they raided and burned villages, sugar plantations, railroad depots and other strategic points, hoping to paralyze the colony. In addition, they were as ruthless as any men fighting in what they considered a just cause: They burned the homes of alleged collaborators with Spain and whipped and killed the accused men. The Spaniards, in turn, adopted a harsh policy, the keystone of which was a reconcentration of the population in the towns firmly held by Spain. In this way the rebels were deprived of food and support from their back-country sympathizers. Consequently the cities became overcrowded prison camps, diseased and hungry.

Nevertheless the rebellion went on; the authorities stepped up the rate of arrests, seizures, searches, tortures and executions. These acts furnished fuel for righteous indignation to an American populace which, in the turbulent years from 1895 to 1898, was itching to find someone with whom it was safe to be angry.

The Cuban uprising occurred just at the time when William Randolph Hearst, then 32, had entered New York City's newspaper publishing wars by acquiring the New York *Journal*. Lavishly using the immense mine and ranch

William Randolph Hearst is here caricatured in the nightgown of the Yellow Kid, a popular comic-strip figure among New Yorkers. When Hearst's "Journal" stole the Yellow Kid's cartoonist from Pulitzer's "World," both papers ran rival Yellow Kid comics. During the ensuing "comics war" between these ruthless competitors, the term "yellow journalism" was coined.

wealth of his father, "Wasteful Willie" had already taken over and made a riotous success of the San Francisco *Examiner*. Now he intended to oust Joseph Pulitzer's New York *World* from its commanding position. Cuba gave Hearst a golden opportunity. It had everything: villains, gore, adventurous gunrunners, high-born maidens laboring for the cause. With such meaty prospects, there was little chance that the *Journal* would choose the more difficult course of trying to explain the revolution to the American people.

The newspapers made Spanish atrocities in Cuba a steady front-page sensation, and as Hearst went, so, inevitably, went Pulitzer. The *Journal* would explain how Spanish troops had resumed "the inhuman practice of beating Cuban prisoners to death," or even drowning them—FEEDING PRISONERS TO SHARKS said the headline. The *World*, not to be outdone, would run a story that described Cuba as a place with "blood on the roadsides, blood in the fields, blood on the doorsteps, blood, blood, blood!"

Day after day the two press barons drummed out the message that liberty-loving Cubans—next-door neighbors—were being massacred and tormented by the evil Spaniards under their commander General Valeriano (or "Butcher") Weyler. Much of the material was written and dispatched northward by imaginative Hearst and Pulitzer employees who never left Havana hotels. The New York papers, in turn, were copied and quoted by other journals throughout the country. Soon, indignation was mounting in the South and West as well as in New York, where the *World* and the *Journal* reached a combined total of more than 1.5 million people daily.

To be sure, Spain was ideally suited for detestation by the vast majority of Americans. Spain was a monarchy. It was Latin rather than Anglo-Saxon and it was Catholic instead of Protestant—these last could have been said of the Cubans as well, but were not. After the divisive emotions of Cleveland's second Administration, Easterners and silver men, Republicans and Bryanites found themselves unified in a growing feeling that it was the nation's moral obligation and historic mission to liberate Cuba.

One major public figure who failed to share the enthusiasm was William McKinley himself. He had no dreams of glory to nurse, and he hoped that Spain could be reasoned into giving up the last of her New World possessions. Moreover, during 1897, business conditions had begun to improve. McKinley, Mark Hanna and spokesmen for the business community as a whole had no desire for a war which could upset the apple cart once more. Far from rubbing their hands over a prospective war boom, financial and commercial journals thought that a Cuban crusade would create inflationary pressures, flutter the stock market, tie up railroad transportation, cause labor shortages and generally be terrible for business.

M CKINLEY and his Cabinet, therefore, made no bold moves. But war fever was rising in Congress. During the closing months of the Cleveland Administration, Congress passed a resolution recognizing Cuban belligerency. Throughout the newspaper-inspired hysteria of 1897, war fever raged on Capitol Hill. In his first annual message, McKinley took cognizance of this sentiment without letting it carry him away.

He deplored the existing state of affairs, lectured Spain on humanity and noted that there had been Spanish promises of reform. Spain, he said, should be given a further chance to end the war on its own. If intervention should

Operating under instructions from Hearst of "You furnish the pictures, I'll furnish the war," artist Frederic Remington caused a national sensation with this drawing of a Cuban girl being searched by three Spaniards on an American ship. Annoyed at being scooped, Pulitzer's "World" soon disclosed that the young woman had really been examined by female officials.

later appear to be necessary, it would be "without fault on our part." The Spanish ambassador in Washington, Enrique Dupuy de Lôme, commented indiscreetly on the message in a letter to a friend in Havana. De Lôme described McKinley as "a common politician who tries to leave a door open behind himself while keeping on good terms with the jingoes of his party." Unfortunately, a rebel spy working in the Havana post office stole the letter and turned it over to insurgent agents in New York, who in turn delivered it to the offices of the New York *Journal*.

While the letter was making its circuitous trip from Washington to Havana to New York, the new American warship *Maine* was ordered to make a "courtesy" call in the port of Havana. Actually the voyage reflected the fears of the nervous United States consul that anti-American rioting might become serious. The *Maine* arrived in the harbor on January 25, 1898, and anchored. Soon after, the De Lôme letter was on its way to Hearst. Both facts were calculated to destroy McKinley's peace policy beyond repair.

On February 9 the *Journal* printed a facsimile of the Spanish ambassador's letter under the blazing head, THE WORST INSULT TO THE UNITED STATES IN ITS HISTORY. (The Cuban supporters, taking no chances, had supplied the text to the rest of the New York press as well.) Forewarned, De Lôme had already submitted his resignation, and the Spanish government apologized in an attempt to avoid the effects of De Lôme's lapse.

On the night of February 15, at 9:40 p.m., there was a tremendous explosion which utterly destroyed the U.S.S. *Maine*. Of the 350 officers and men aboard, 260 died. The proud vessel was transformed into a sunken coffin of twisted metal. An American court of inquiry convened; it judged that a submarine mine had been set off, which in turn blew up the ship's forward magazines. Spanish investigators insisted that the explosion was internal. It did not matter. Even if a mine had sunk the *Maine*, there was no conceivable way of finding out who had placed it against the hull, or how or why. To this day the sinking remains a mystery.

No doubts troubled the press and the jingoes. THE WARSHIP MAINE WAS SPLIT IN TWO BY AN ENEMY'S SECRET INFERNAL MACHINE, screamed the *Journal* of February 17, and the story made it clear that the enemy was Spain. The next day the headline proclaimed: THE WHOLE COUNTRY THRILLS WITH THE WAR FEVER. This was the most truthful report the *Journal* had run in some time. Under the slogan of "Remember the *Maine!* To hell with Spain!" the nation surged toward war.

Charles Vernon Gridley, who commanded the "Olympia," flagship of the Asiatic Squadron, was pronounced physically unfit for active duty just before the battle of Manila Bay. He insisted on staying at his post and received Dewey's celebrated command: "You may fire when you are ready, Gridley."

THE Spanish themselves had done their best to avoid it. Between September of 1897 and April of 1898, Madrid had recalled General Weyler, offered autonomy to Cuba, freed American prisoners captured while aiding the rebels and even revoked the reconcentration order. The American minister cabled the State Department in Washington at the end of March, "Public opinion in Spain has moved steadily toward peace," and he begged for more time to negotiate. On April 9 the Spanish even agreed to an armistice in Cuba. A strong President might have taken this complete victory to the public and made a fight for peace. Instead, on Monday, April 11, McKinley asked Congress to give him war powers and said: "I await your action."

Everyone knew what the action would be. On the 19th, Congress declared Cuba independent and authorized McKinley to use the army and navy to guarantee that independence. In a spasm of idealism the legislators added an amendment proposed by Senator Henry M. Teller of Colorado that disclaimed any intention to claim sovereignty, jurisdiction or control over Cuba. The next day McKinley demanded that Spain leave Cuba, and when the expected rupture of diplomatic relations followed, Congress voted a state of war on April 25. The hour of the expansionists, the big-navy men and the warmakers had finally come.

A MERICA fought the war with zest, clumsiness, gallantry and incredible good luck. Within a week the country had a smashing victory at sea and a naval hero. In a bizarre opening to a curious war, this battle took place not in Cuban waters, but halfway around the world in the Philippine Islands, which even McKinley had to locate by looking them up on a globe. As Finley Peter Dunne's "Mr. Dooley" put it, the American people did not know whether the Philippines "were islands or canned goods."

Early in 1898 the small American Asiatic squadron commanded by Commodore George Dewey had received orders to coal up and lay in wait at Hong Kong. If and when war broke out, Dewey was to see to it that a Spanish naval force based at Manila did not leave Asian waters.

Before dawn on May 1, the light cruisers and gunboats of Dewey's squadron steamed into the harbor at Manila past inexplicably, incredibly silent Spanish shore batteries on Corregidor Island. The six American vessels found a larger (but less powerfully gunned) Spanish force at anchor. At 5:40 Dewey gave his flagship commander, Charles Vernon Gridley, the historic order to fire when ready. At 7:35 the Spanish ships, whose fire had been wildly inaccurate, were almost completely silenced and at least three were in flames. Dewey's force quietly drew out of range for breakfast. At 11:00 the American ships moved in again to smash the shore batteries. That evening the fleet was anchored off Manila, its bands playing "the usual evening concert."

The cost of wiping out Spanish sea power in the Pacific had been eight men slightly wounded. Dewey cabled the news back home and waited for the arrival of troops to enable him to occupy the city. The message had to be taken to Hong Kong before it could be transmitted, so Washington did not receive it until May 7, whereupon the country went noisily mad. Dewey was voted a promotion, an elaborate sword, a Congressional vote of thanks. Babies, yachts, race horses and dogs were named after him, and business was brisk in souvenirs bearing his likeness.

The war's opening victory caused a sudden outburst of national unity, perhaps best symbolized by two previously implacable political enemies, "Pitchfork Ben" Tillman and Mark Hanna (now a senator), companionably riding in the same carriage after receiving the news at the Navy Department.

The country, in fact, was bubbling with unity. Bryan, appointed Colonel of the Third Nebraska Volunteers, was ready to do his duty under McKinley's orders. And William Allen White, whose editorial thrusts at Populism had done much to defeat Bryan, declared in language that was reminiscent of Bryan's grandiloquent prose: "War . . . is one of God's weapons for fighting the devil in man. Therefore we welcome God's chastening hand."

Into the blue uniform of a volunteer cavalry general rushed a scarecrow-thin, white-bearded 61-year-old gamecock, "Fighting Joe" Wheeler. It was later claimed that during a battle with the Spaniards, Wheeler, who had been

Army Lieutenant Andrew S. Rowan wrote such a good book about Cuba that nobody realized he had never been there. So he drew the risky job of taking a message to the insurgent General García behind the Spanish lines. Rowan's heroism was finally rewarded by a grateful nation 24 years later.

a distinguished Confederate cavalry commander, cried out in confusion, "We've got the damn Yankees on the run!" But his presence in the army helped complete the reconciliation of North and South.

If Wheeler was the most colorful contribution of the Democrats to the war, the Republicans made theirs in Lieutenant-Colonel Theodore Roosevelt of the First United States Volunteer Cavalry, better known as the "Rough Riders." For Roosevelt the war was "bully." Though he was not quite 40 when it came, he had already done a good deal of living. He had been a New York state legislator, unsuccessful candidate for New York City mayor, a civil-service commissioner under Harrison and Cleveland, and president of New York City's police commission.

He had also owned a ranch in the Dakotas, helped ride herd on his own cattle, shot big game in the Rockies and recorded the experiences in books. He had several respectable volumes of history to his credit. In 1897 McKinley had paid a small debt to New York Republican leaders by making Roosevelt Assistant Secretary of the Navy. During his tenure Roosevelt had spoken up enthusiastically for various projects dear to Alfred T. Mahan and Roosevelt's own good friend, Henry Cabot Lodge: a big fleet, a transoceanic canal through Central America, the acquisition of Hawaii and war to free Cuba. When the war finally came, Roosevelt was given permission, along with Leonard Wood, a regular army surgeon of combative tastes, to organize a mounted outfit—Wood to command, Roosevelt to be his assistant.

The unit that emerged was composed of a curious combination of Roosevelt's admirers—tough Western cowpokes and socialites from the best Eastern colleges and clubs. T.R. was far more newsworthy than was Leonard Wood, and thanks to his presence, the regiment drew an inordinate share of newspaper attention, considering that it numbered fewer than 1,000 of the 223,000 men who enlisted for the war. But in its vigorous amateurism, the regiment did present a fairly accurate indication of the character of the entire volunteer army of 1898. What was more, it got to do some fighting.

For there was land fighting to do. The country demanded an expedition to

CUBA: AMATEURS WIN A WAR

On June 22-23, 1898, 17,000 raw U.S. troops landed at Daiquiri and Siboney and pushed toward Las Guásimas, following the retreating Spanish (dotted lines). El Caney fell on July 1; that same day 8,000 men forced their way up San Juan Hill. Now Santiago, the main Spanish stronghold, was surrounded. The naval force that the Spaniards had hoped would bring reinforcements was blockaded in Santiago harbor; when it tried to escape, American ships met and destroyed the Spanish vessels. Although the Spaniards did receive some reinforcements, the American siege forced their surrender. On July 17 the war in Cuba was over.

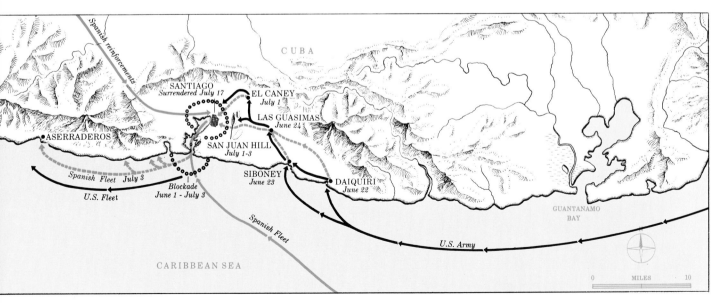

Cuba, and the War Department, with no experience in the previous 33 years aside from organizing Indian campaigns, tried to bring the soldiers to combat efficiency. A Fifth Army Corps, under the 300-pound General William Shafter, was created and assembled at Tampa, Florida. The confusion was indescribable; half-trained regiments were sent to destinations miles away from their baggage, tents and equipment.

Clad in woolen winter uniforms—for nothing else was provided—troops drilled under a hot Florida sun for almost six weeks, while the United States Navy cautiously looked for the Spanish Atlantic squadron of Admiral Pascual Cervera. His four armored cruisers and three destroyers were supposedly prowling the Atlantic, waiting their chance to dart in to shell New York, Boston, Philadelphia or other American coastal towns. In point of fact Admiral Cervera's force had left the Cape Verde Islands in a woeful state of unpreparedness and was badly handicapped by a short supply of coal. The admiral had finally slipped into Cuba's Santiago harbor on May 19, under the nose of the United States fleet.

Ten days later the Americans discovered this fact, and the navy announced that it was ready to convoy transports to Cuba. Thereupon Shafter issued orders to some 17,000 men, including 89 correspondents and artists and photographers. Eighteen regular infantry and two volunteer infantry regiments, five regular cavalry and one volunteer cavalry outfit—the Rough Riders—bid goodby to hotels, barrooms and newspaper interviewers in Florida and marched down to board some 32 coastal transports assembled to carry them.

In the photograph above, General Joseph ("Fighting Joe") Wheeler, who had a fine record as a Confederate cavalryman in the Civil War, wears his Rebel uniform. Later he was a political leader in Alabama and a member of Congress. A firm advocate of reconciliation between North and South, he volunteered at 61 for the Spanish-American War and wore Union blue (below).

THE embarkation on June 7 was a scene of even worse confusion than was the training. Regiments fought for possession of available ships. The one railroad track to the Tampa docks was quickly clogged; units were transported and loaded in whatever way possible, and vast quantities of essential equipment—including most of the cavalry horses, for which there was no room anyway—were left behind. Then the whole expedition sweltered at anchor for a week until the navy decided to sail.

On June 22 part of this force went ashore near the town of Daiquiri, 18 miles east of Santiago. The only landing craft were small boats that ferried the troops from the transports to a thoroughly inadequate pier jutting out from an open beach. The few horses—officers' mounts and draft animals—were pushed overboard to swim in, encouraged by buglers who blew assembly calls from the beach. A day or so later the rest of the Fifth Corps disembarked at Siboney, eight miles farther west.

The Spaniards, who had over 150,000 regulars in Cuba and ultimately assembled 14,000 men in Santiago, were providentially inept. In addition they were demoralized and hungry after long months of fighting guerrillas. By June 24, when "Fighting Joe" Wheeler pushed ahead toward Santiago and had a sharp little skirmish at Las Guásimas, the American beachhead was safe—at least from the Spanish.

Then followed a campaign whose actual fighting phase was confined to some 10 days: of those, the most crucial was July 1. As Shafter closed in on Santiago, he came up against two key Spanish positions—at the village of El Caney and on a ridge known as San Juan Hill, where blockhouses defended the heights which dominated the city itself. The attack on El Caney, on the right of the American line, was a tough daylong affair. The positions of the

THE LIBERATORS
TURN TO CONQUEST

On December 21, 1898, McKinley ordered troops occupying Manila to seize the entire Philippines. Unwilling to trade Spanish for American rule, Emilio Aguinaldo led a rebellion. By October 1899 the insurgents had been defeated at Manila, Malolos and Iloilo. After new losses at Vigan, Tacloban and Barceloneta, Aguinaldo turned to guerrilla action, staging bloody raids at Loculan, Tinuba and Santa Cruz. But Aguinaldo's capture at Palanan in 1901 discouraged the rebels, and after a few skirmishes, including one at Gandara, peace was concluded on July 4, 1902.

Spanish riflemen, who used smokeless powder, were concealed from the Americans. Still using old-fashioned powder, the Americans gave themselves away with huge clouds of white smoke every time they fired.

In front of San Juan Hill, a dangerous situation developed as more than 8,000 Americans tried to move into position over narrow jungle trails, constantly raked by Spanish fire from high ground ahead. To make matters worse, an observation balloon floated over their heads, pinpointing them amid the heavy vegetation. Roosevelt, now in command of the Rough Riders, found himself and his men pinned down around noon in front of a height later known as Kettle Hill.

Retreat would have been a sheer disaster considering the congested trail behind. To sit tight was an equally risky course. Roosevelt, whose bravery was genuine (his only real fear was that he would lose his glasses in action and be helpless; he had a dozen extra pairs stuffed in various parts of his uniform), waved his hand for an advance. The Rough Riders and a mixed lot of soldiers who had drifted in from other units—including a number of unsung Negro regulars, troopers from the nearby 9th and 10th Cavalry—went up with a rush. The public was later to become confused by Roosevelt's own self-dramatization and regard this incident as the charge which captured San Juan Hill, won Santiago and showed that Roosevelt was the master of the day. At the time the action was relatively meaningless, except to demonstrate the ex-Assistant Secretary's own gallantry, get some troops out of a hole and move the American positions forward.

By July 3 El Caney and San Juan Hill were in American hands, but the casualties of about 1,500—10 per cent of the entire force—were not encouraging. That morning the Spaniards themselves went proudly to destruction. Admiral Cervera led his little fleet out of Santiago harbor, turned westward and attempted to dodge past the waiting American force. Four American battleships, plus other vessels, gave chase and gradually overhauled him. By late afternoon all the Spanish ships had run aground or blown up or surrendered. As one of Cervera's officers put it, the opening gun of that day was "the signal that the history of four centuries of grandeur was at an end."

Spain, which had found the New World, was leaving it. The next day the officer in charge, Admiral William T. Sampson, begged to present Cervera's fleet as a Fourth of July present to the nation—a somewhat flawed offer, since Sampson had been miles away while the victory was being won by Commodore Winfield S. Schley. Nevertheless Sampson's wire to Washington set off Manila Bay celebrations once more.

THE destruction of Cervera's fleet meant that Cuba could not be reinforced and must fall. On July 17 Santiago was formally surrendered. It happened none too soon, for the Americans who had escaped Spanish bullets were beginning to fall victim to disease as they lay in the muddy siegeworks. Malaria, typhoid and dysentery raged. Yellow fever was appearing. On July 27 the sick list numbered 4,122. Doctors, themselves ill with fever, had to make do with meager supplies, improvised hospitals and an insufficient number of ambulances to transport the soldiers.

Unless a proper base could be built at Santiago at once, the army would waste away by sickness or starvation. By late July, however, the warriors who had freed Cuba in such hot blood were equally impatient to get home.

Unwilling to face political unpleasantness in an election year, the government packed the troops at Santiago aboard transports once more, landed them at another jerry-built temporary camp at the tip of Long Island in mid-August and had most of them mustered out within a few weeks.

Those who had fought had gotten their bellies full of blood and horror and boredom. To them the war would never have the comic-opera overtones which later generations were to perceive. Yet the adventure had lasted only four months for most of the volunteers—about the length of a college summer vacation. And the results were prodigious for the effort expended.

That was why John Hay, soon to be Secretary of State, was able to write to his friend Roosevelt: "It has been a splendid little war; begun with the highest motives, carried on with magnificent intelligence and spirit, favored by that fortune which loves the brave." But a young reporter-artist, Charles J. Post, who had fought with the 71st New York Volunteers and returned to Manhattan a fever-ridden skeleton, had a more terse way of summing up the experience. "I was lucky," he wrote. "I had survived." *(See page 140.)*

T HE nation, too, had survived its own haste and excitement. The harsh criticisms of the War Department were not wholly fair. Considering the vast amount of planning, training, staging and construction that should have gone into a waterborne invasion, the miracle was that an army corps swept together in four or five weeks and simply dumped on a Cuban beach performed as well as it did. Rather than considering itself merely lucky, however, the United States assumed that its victories proved its ineffable might. America was convinced that it should act the role of imperial greatness into which it had stumbled.

The Spanish helped by putting up no further resistance. At the end of July American troops arrived to secure Manila. Meanwhile another American force had landed, virtually without opposition, on Puerto Rico. On August 12 the Spanish, after approaching the United States through the French ambassador, signed a preliminary peace yielding control of Cuba and promising to cede Puerto Rico and one of the tiny Marianas Islands in the Pacific as war damages. Spain also permitted American occupation of Manila until a final treaty of peace should be concluded.

The country settled down during the summer to decide what it wanted in the pending negotiations. It was then that a remarkable polarization of public opinion occurred. On the one hand there were the frank imperialists of the prewar days—men like Lodge and Roosevelt who held that the United States could do no less than pick up the fallen remnants of the Spanish Empire. Fact as well as theory were now on their side, for America was already lodged in the Philippines and thus in Asia.

Indeed, the Hawaiian annexation plan had once again been placed before the House in May, during the excitement following Dewey's victory. The argument that America should bridge the Pacific—that is, put a halfway house between California and the Philippines—was joined with others to carry the day. This time there was no treaty needing a two thirds vote. A simple joint resolution of annexation, signed by McKinley on July 7, did the trick.

But Hawaii was not Puerto Rico, nor was it the Philippines. Hawaii was already run by a dominant American-descended class of businessmen. This was not the case in the Philippines. The Filipinos, grateful for liberation from

PUNGENT CRITICISM BY A BARROOM PHILOSOPHER

In 1893 a Chicago newspaperman, Finley Peter Dunne, created "Mr. Dooley," an Irish-American saloonkeeper whose caustic commentary amused all Americans—even its victims. After Dunne's criticism (below) of Roosevelt's history of the Rough Riders, T.R. wrote to him: "I regret to state that my family and intimate friends are delighted with your review of my book."

"This here book . . . fell fr'm th' lips iv Tiddy Rosenfelt. . . . 'I r-ran into th' entire military force iv th' United States lying on its stomach . . . . I sint th' ar-rmy home an' attackted San Joon hill. Ar-rmed on'y with a small thirty-two . . . I climbed that precipitous ascent in th' face iv th' most gallin' fire I iver knew or heerd iv. . . . They has been some discussion as to who was th' first man to r-reach th' summit iv San Joon hill. . . . I will say f'r th' binifit iv posterity that I was th' on'y man I see. An' I had a tillyscope.' I have thried, Hinnissy," Mr. Dooley continued, "to give you a fair idee iv th' contints iv this remarkable book. . . . If I was him I'd call th' book 'Alone in Cubia.' "

"I don't know what to do with th' Ph'lippeens . . . . We can't sell thim, we can't ate thim, an' . . . 'twud be a disgrace f'r to lave befure we've pounded these frindless an' ongrateful people into insinsibility. . . . They'se wan consolation; and that is, if th' American people can govern thimsilves, they can govern annything that walks."

"We're a gr-reat people," said Mr. Hennessy, earnestly. "We ar-re," said Mr. Dooley. "We ar-re that. An' th' best iv it is, we know we ar-re."

"An' so th' war is over?" asked Mr. Hennessy. "On'y part iv it," said Mr. Dooley. "Th' part that ye see in th' pitcher pa-apers is over, but th' tax collector will continyoo his part iv th' war with relentless fury."

Spain, showed no interest in accepting rule by Americans. Troop units which had sailed to fight the Spaniards found themselves for the next three years in the awkward position of shooting at the natives instead—doing precisely what the Spanish themselves had done in Cuba.

Opponents of the imperialists gradually became more outspoken and organized an Anti-Imperialist League which attracted numerous adherents. Grover Cleveland and Andrew Carnegie were members, and so were John Sherman (McKinley's first Secretary of State) and Samuel Gompers. It was an oddly assorted group, drawing strength both from its respectability and from the efforts of members and nonmembers—among them William Graham Sumner, William Dean Howells and Mark Twain—who wrote vigorously anti-imperialist pamphlets.

The idealistic opponents of imperialism said that it would be a sin for the United States to end a war for liberation of a heroic people by making itself the master of subject millions. Racists among the anti-imperialists argued that the creation of an American empire embracing black- and brown-skinned "non-Anglo-Saxons" would spell doom: They could never be admitted to self-government; to hold them in subjugation would require a massive standing army, a perennial threat to liberty; they would be imported to debase American workers' wages. America would do best to emulate the lean, agrarian and soldierly virtues of the Roman Republic, and not the expensive vices of the Roman Empire. That way lay decline and fall.

The imperialists, however, had picked up new recruits over the summer. Businessmen who had dreaded the war now sensed possibilities and opportunities in an empire. Perhaps it would be wise to get established in Asia—whose teeming millions would some day need leather, tobacco, soap and lamps—before the Germans or Japanese or British closed it off.

Mark Hanna decided that the Chinese market alone was worth keeping open, and the Philippines might be the necessary lever. "If it is commercialism to want possession of a strategic point giving the American people an opportunity to maintain a foothold in the markets of that great Eastern country," he declared with characteristic directness, "for God's sake let's have commercialism." Others, less forthright, wanted a more moral foundation for expansion. It was not hard for them to find spokesmen in the pulpit.

A New England Methodist minister, who was undoubtedly voicing the sentiments of thousands of clergymen and churchgoers, said, "I'm proud of my country in Cuba and Porto Rico . . . patiently teaching the people to govern themselves, and to enjoy the blessings of Christian civilization. . . . Surely this Spanish war has not been a grab for empire, but an heroic effort [to] free the oppressed, and to teach the millions of ignorant, debased human beings thus freed how to live."

In the end it was this argument that proved irresistible to President McKinley, who held the key to the situation. In October he instructed the peace commissioners to demand cession of the Philippines. As he explained later to a visiting clerical delegation:

> I walked the floor of the White House night after night until midnight; and I am not ashamed to tell you, gentlemen, that I went down on my knees and prayed Almighty God for light and guidance more than one night. And one night it came to me this way—I don't know how it was, but it came: (1) That we

Emilio Aguinaldo, leader of the Philippine insurgents, joined U.S. forces in the fighting for Manila but ended up, as shown here, a prisoner aboard a U.S. gunboat. Aguinaldo claimed he had been promised Philippine independence, and attacked American troops when it was withheld. Renouncing bloodshed, he lived to see his people achieve autonomy in 1946.

could not give them back to Spain—that would be cowardly and dishonorable; (2) that we would not turn them over to France or Germany—our commercial rivals in the Orient—that would be bad business and discreditable; (3) that we could not leave them to themselves—they were unfit for self-government—and they would soon have anarchy and misrule over there worse than Spain's was; and (4) that there was nothing left for us to do but to take them all, and to educate the Filipinos, and uplift and civilize and Christianize them, and by God's grace to do the best we could by them. . . . And then I went to bed, and went to sleep, and slept soundly, and the next morning I sent for the chief engineer of the War Department (our map-maker) and I told him to put the Philippines on the map of the United States . . . and there they are. . . .

McKINLEY, early in May, could not have told "within 2,000 miles" where the Philippines were. Seldom has anyone recorded the change that took place in five months in the minds of millions of Americans so clearly as the President in his account of his midnight soul-searching.

True, William Jennings Bryan, who had a tendency to believe that he heard the divine word a bit more clearly than did others, had now come out as an anti-imperialist, hoping that opposition to empire would be a useful issue in 1900. He was wrong; McKinley beat him in 1900 by an even wider margin than in 1896.

So, in February 1899, the Senate passed the peace treaty that acquired the Philippines, Puerto Rico and Guam (one of the Marianas Islands). During that year America divided the Samoan Islands with Germany and took possession of Wake Island as well. Also in 1899 Secretary of State John Hay asked Berlin, London and St. Petersburg, Tokyo, Rome and Paris to agree to the so-called "Open Door" policy, whereby all the great powers would guarantee equal commercial opportunity within their spheres of influence in China. And in the following year, when a group of anti-foreign Chinese, the "Boxers," staged an uprising in Peking and penned up the European colony in its legations, 2,500 American soldiers took part in an international military rescue operation (the Chinese government itself being powerless).

It was done. Not entirely at the urgings of Mahan and Strong—certainly not to satisfy American investors or traders with foreign nations—the United States had become a nation with overseas possessions, with all the grandeurs and miseries attached. Cuba, idealism, naval technology, religion, fate and the urge for relief from the tensions of the '90s—all had played a part in bringing about the change.

William Allen White put it most simply. "What is to be will be," he said, adding a wistful note: "And yet thousands of people cannot help longing for the old order. They cannot but feel that . . . this deepening of responsibilities brings a hardship with it. . . ." "Mr. Dooley," less sentimental, simply announced that as "a wurruld power" we could no longer watch quietly while others played the game of international poker. We were now a part of it, and "be Hivins, we have no peace iv mind."

It would take a while for the full meaning of such warnings to sink in. But as the Stars and Stripes went up over Manila and Honolulu and San Juan, Americans were not apt to take a somber view. They stood on the threshold of a new century, at the gateway of a new world. They had made more of the world theirs, and most of them were exuberant. It was a time for looking at where they had come from, and for choosing new destinations.

This cartoon from the cover of the old "Life" magazine for December 28, 1899, was captioned: "Our Expansive Uncle But It's Only Temporary." It was a wry comment on the widely held view that the will of providence ("Manifest Destiny") compelled the United States to expand beyond its borders, even at the cost of war, to save less fortunate peoples from barbarism.

A bad summer for an amateur army

THE *Maine* was a tangled wreck in the harbor of Havana. . . . We commoner folk began to boil and seethe with ardor to kill a Spaniard." Thus Charles J. Post launched his memoir of the Cuban campaign. As a knowledgeable New Yorker and newspaper artist, Post realized that publisher William Randolph Hearst had incited the war and was boosting circulation by inciting patriotism. Nevertheless Post enlisted in the 71st Infantry Regiment of the New York National Guard. As an inconspicuous private he fought as well as most, traded sketches for food and survived "Compound-Enteric-Typhoid-Malaria" to paint the vivid combat pictures on the following pages.

Private Post's little war had more than its fair share of comic confusions, tragic mistakes and bizarre anomalies. Fighting cheek by jowl, without modern arms or decent maps, were an ex-Confederate general, Joe Wheeler, and a young man who would become Secretary of the Navy in World War II, Frank Knox. Time and again the army was rescued from disaster by an enemy just as incompetent, and dispirited to boot. Colonel Teddy Roosevelt damned the level of American generalship at San Juan Hill *(opposite)*, saying, "The battle simply fought itself." Later Post reached the same conclusion about the strategy of the entire campaign: "It had none." But the amateur private, more generous than the amateur colonel, summed up: "It was a commando raid long before the term 'commando' had been invented . . . a brilliant military victory . . . against odds and in spite of blunders on the very battle line!"

INVITING WAR, the armored U.S. cruiser *Maine* glides past Morro Castle into Havana harbor on January 25, 1898. War came two months after the ship was blown up on February 15.

SCRAMBLING TO VICTORY up San Juan Hill *(opposite)*, U.S. troops escape a deadly barrage, and storm the hilltop blockhouse. This key to Santiago's defenses fell on July 1, 1898.

140

EMBARKING FOR CUBA, the brash Rough Riders commandeer a transport intended for other troops. In the foreground stands their famed dynamite gun, which fired an explosive torpedo.

Muddles and blunders from Florida to Cuban shores

ILL-FED and sweltering in winter woolens, the invasion army slowly assembled and haphazardly drilled in Florida's snake-infested palmetto scrub. Early in June, amid scenes of wild confusion, some 17,000 troops and 3,000 animals boarded 32 transports at Tampa *(left)*. There they stewed for a week awaiting orders.

The invasion itself, luckily unopposed, began in just such disorder east of Santiago. Scrambling ashore at Daiquiri, the Rough Riders impatiently headed inland to seek combat. A day later Private Post's 71st New York landed at Siboney just in time to rush to the Rough Riders' relief. Arriving breathless, his company heard some shots, saw a few wounded, but the skirmish was over. "The march back was all gaiety," said Post. In Siboney, among their gathering allies *(opposite)*, he added, "Cuban insurgents looked at us, and we felt that now we were their equals—we too had been under fire!"

Army horses and mules, shoved overboard when unloading craft proved inadequate, swim for the Cuban shore. Some panicked and drowned.

RAGTAG REBELS, veterans of Cuba's three-year war for independence from Spain, lope along behind General Calixto García on their way to join the Americans. Guerrilla bands like this one specialized in ambushes outside the Spaniards' city strongholds. Post said of them, "Barefoot, or only in rawhide sandals, they could outmarch any of the professional armies."

Below San Juan Hill, Americans reel under savage fire at Bloody Ford. At left a dying colonel is carried from the stream in an abandoned

At Bloody Ford, a harrowing prelude to San Juan Hill

ON July 1 nearly 8,000 U.S. troops closed in on Santiago's hill defenses. As they reached the stream below San Juan Hill, converging enemy fire turned the narrow ford into a deathtrap for hundreds. Lieutenant John J. Pershing and his troop of Negro 10th Cavalry stood in waist-deep water "awaiting the order to deploy . . . under this galling fire of exploding shrapnel and deadly mauser volleys." Post and his New York Infantry

GATLING GUNS hauled by mules *(left)* arrive to turn the tide at San Juan Hill. After conventional artillery failed, the four rapid-fire guns dislodged Spanish defenders and covered the U.S. attackers.

WOUNDED TROOPS take shelter *(right)* behind the captured San Juan blockhouse. At left, other Americans continue the battle, firing over Spanish corpses in white and their dead comrades in blue.

chair. Behind the column at right, Post himself is stumbling along.

floundered at Bloody Ford *(above)*, victims of their own general who "had broken the plan of attack and deflected it into complete confusion." The 71st cheered Roosevelt *(right)* as the Rough Riders pushed past them, but Teddy snapped back, "Don't cheer, but fight, now's the time to fight." That afternoon gallantry overcame disorganization. At random, intermixed outfits rushed up San Juan Hill, seized the blockhouse *(below)* and won the war.

Wearing Rough Rider khaki,
Colonel Teddy Roosevelt
"looked as if he had slept in it."

A MISERABLE LOT, men of the 71st fry up a soggy meal during the 16-day siege of Santiago. Food and medicine were in short supply; tents were often flooded and aswarm with mosquitoes.

In siege and victory, ordeals of fever and despair

AFTER the loss of San Juan Hill, Santiago braced for siege. Two days later, on July 3, its bottled-up fleet made a dash for freedom and got pounded to scrap. On July 15 its authorities made their formal surrender.

But by then the Americans had little to cheer about. The heavy summer rains had begun, spreading dysentery, malaria, typhoid and yellow fever. Thousands fell sick. Post and the 71st New York, sprawling in the dismal bivouac they called Misery Hill (above), watched helpless as litter-bearers and burial details went their grim rounds. Then the generals forced the issue with a public warning that "This Army must be moved at once or it will perish as an Army." By mid-August the ravaged victors struggled into Santiago, onto transports bound for home. The war, if not the dying, had ended.

A VICTORIOUS RABBLE, veterans of the 71st New York strut through Cuba. They were scrawny, tattered and malodorous. "But one thing," said Post, "we did look tough."

146

7. THE EVE OF THE NEW CENTURY

As 1899 wound toward its close, editors reviewed the century just passing. The New York *Times* struck the general note. The 19th Century, it observed, had been "marked by greater progress in all that pertains to the material well-being and enlightenment of mankind than all the previous history of the race; and the political, social, and moral advancement has been hardly less striking." The century's scientific achievements, the *Times* went on, "relegate all the science that preceded . . . to the same category as the lore of the Chaldaeans and the Egyptians." It was a source of particular pride to note that, at this triumphant moment, the United States was helping to carry "the regenerating forces of popular government to the uttermost parts of the earth."

On such a tide of confidence—perhaps arrogance is the word—America surged into the new era. The same current raised high the fortunes of the Republican party, which was given credit for uplifting the heathen, rebuking the tyrant, guaranteeing progress and restoring prosperity. And prosperity was returning, for a variety of reasons. Among them were a small 1897 wheat crop in Europe, which boosted world prices, and a quickened demand for American industrial products, which pushed our total exports to over $1 billion—a figure well in excess of the value of imports that year.

With this favorable balance of trade, gold began to flow into the country. From 1897 on, a lusty little gold rush in the Klondike had helped to increase

CONFIDENT LEADER, William McKinley radiates dignity. He was a skillful leader too; implacable foes would often leave his office together, with smiles on their faces.

The New York "Evening Journal" featured these two cartoons during the election campaign of 1900. Above, "Willie" McKinley, shown as the Trusts' little boy, plays with his roughriding running mate Teddy Roosevelt. "Nursie," who is Republican party boss Mark Hanna, complacently watches. Below, Nursie squelches bumptious Teddy, while Willie jumps with glee.

the supply of that metal. It also gave the country its last real taste of a hell-raising frontier. Further world gold strikes and continued export surpluses combined, by 1900, to make the silver issue a political fossil. In 1900 McKinley's Administration put the country on the gold standard. The Populist strength in the House had sunk to seven in 1898. Populist state administrations gradually disappeared, as the voters returned to their old party homes in various degrees of contrition.

Neither silver nor the tariff provided campaign issues. In 1897 the Republicans in Congress enacted the Dingley Tariff, which raised rates to an average of 52 per cent, yet they kept control of Congress the next year. Too late, Bryan tried to peg the 1900 campaign to anti-imperialism. Mark Hanna had the electorate on his side when he declared: "There is only one issue in this campaign, my friends, and that is, let well enough alone." McKinley won, more easily than in 1896. Conservatism seemed to have carried the day.

YET there were qualifications to the victory of "letting well enough alone." McKinley's running mate was Theodore Roosevelt. Nationally famous after the Spanish-American War, Roosevelt had been elected governor of New York. In office he proved too dynamic for Republican boss Tom Platt, who avoided a second Albany term for "T.R." by getting him nominated for the vice presidency. Roosevelt had misgivings about entering such a political tomb —and so, it is alleged, did Mark Hanna, who reportedly asked a group of delegates: "Don't any of you realize that there's only one life between that madman and the Presidency?" But Roosevelt's presence on the ticket indicated the emergence of a new generation of Republican leadership. When McKinley, a veteran of the Civil War, had run for his first congressional term in 1876, Roosevelt had been a Harvard freshman. Now T.R. and his contemporaries were moving in on the party's centers of power, trying to re-apply its earlier moral zeal to the perplexities of the new era.

The Vice President was still an exuberant, intemperate young politician, rich in color and correct sentiments, but with no visible program. Soon he would be spokesman and hero for a new breed of young Republicans—and Democrats—eager to end boss control of parties, provide cities with clean and efficient government, curb railroads and trusts, and conserve the nation's resources. His expansionism and his war record already identified him with America's new, adventurous status in the international arena.

Roosevelt's election to the vice presidency—unimportant as was the office itself—meant that the voters had not voted themselves quite so much conservatism as they expected. And there were also the more than six million Democrats whose votes for Bryan had endorsed a man who, in his own way, stood for changes in the social and economic patterns of the '90s.

So there were stirrings, even amidst the contentment of prosperity and expansion. The country wanted progress; it also wanted ideals and equality. It could not get them all without some fresh political thought.

Progress—and consolidation—seemed to move on irresistibly. In 1899, business mergers numbering 1,208 were reported, as against 303 the year before and only 69 in 1897. In 1901, the gigantic United States Steel Corporation was created, partly because Andrew Carnegie was ready to sell out for some $492 million and also because J. Pierpont Morgan, eager to avoid a fierce trade war in steel, agreed to assist in financing a merger.

U.S. Steel merged 12 of the largest companies then in existence, whose assets numbered scores of blast furnaces, steelworks and rolling mills; thousands of acres of ore, coal and limestone lands; more than 100 steamships and a thousand miles of railroad. The new corporation could produce some eight million tons of finished steel a year. It supplied over half of the country's requirements for steel rails and structural steel, and most of its nails and barbed wire. Capitalized at $1.4 billion, it was created shortly after the 10th birthday of the Sherman Antitrust Act.

Combination had proceeded very rapidly during the late '90s. The Census of Manufacturers of 1900 counted 185 huge corporations that controlled 2,040 plants, provided jobs for 8 per cent of the workers and produced about 14 per cent of the goods made in their respective lines in the United States. The tightness of the control varied with the field. For example, textile corporations in this top echelon made less than 4.5 per cent of all cloth. But the steel companies in the group made 28.5 and the chemical firms 33.5 per cent of the nation's output; the distillers, 22 per cent of the liquor; and the Westinghouse and General Electric companies, between them, controlled all the country's apparatus for electric power transmission.

The railroads, shaken by the 1893 depression, were being bunched together like stray cattle under the prodding of the great banking houses. Between July 1899 and November 1900, some 25,000 miles of road went into new combinations. By 1906, two thirds of the total national network of 225,000 miles would be woven into seven great systems, five of them under Vanderbilt, Morgan, Gould, Hill, Harriman—names spoken in awed whispers. (The Gould and the Vanderbilt were the heirs of the Jay Gould and the old Commodore who had waged such Homeric contests in the '60s.)

It was a big country, and its lords of industry thought and traded in huge figures—billions, in fact—though much of the capitalization of the new corporations represented future earning power, not current assets.

The question was: Who would run America? And how? The dynamo, the locomotive, the blast furnace had created a new kind of force in human affairs. In America, how could this productive might be preserved for its acknowledged good yet reconciled with individual liberty? The problem, at root, was one of power. The history of the new century would be one of power and the struggle for its control.

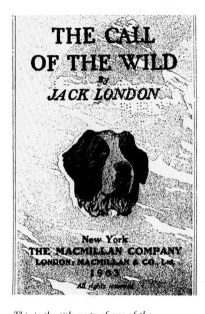

This is the title page of one of the most popular adventure stories of the Klondike gold-rush days of the late '90s. The author, Jack London, went prospecting in Alaska and later wrote up his experiences. The book tells of a dog named Buck, who was kidnaped and shipped to Alaska. There he hearkened to "The Call of the Wild" and ran off with a pack of wolves.

THE sounds of a new kind of power were audible on city streets in 1900. The popping and belching of the automobile was becoming a part of the urban scene, though the gasoline engine was just beginning to fight it out with steam and electricity for the job of replacing the horse. In 1900, of 4,192 automobiles manufactured, 1,681 were steamers, 1,575 were electrics and 936 were powered by what the census called "hydrocarbon."

But the pattern was set. On a bitter-cold Thanksgiving Day in 1895, a "motocycle" race sponsored by a Chicago newspaper over a 52-mile course was won by a "buggyaut," the work of two brothers, Charles and Frank Duryea, recently Massachusetts bicycle makers. It looked like—and was—a four-wheeled buggy, powered by a two-cylinder gasoline engine and steered by a tiller. Through the drifted snow it bucked and snorted, pursued by laughing spectators in horse-drawn sleighs and cutters, completing the 52-mile stint at an average speed of just over five miles per hour.

Another mechanically minded young man, Henry Ford, was constructing a gasoline engine in Detroit, where he was chief engineer for the Detroit Edison Company. The story goes that in 1896 Ford talked with Thomas Edison. The old wizard advised Ford to stick with gasoline. "Electric cars must keep near to power stations. The storage battery is too heavy. Steam cars . . . have to have a boiler and fire. . . . You have the thing. Keep at it." Ford did, and so did others, with consequences that would remake American life. One change —a grim one—was a report in the Chicago *Tribune* of December 31, 1899, that an electric "auto cab" had run down a pedestrian, the first victim of such an accident in the city, it was claimed.

A more spectacular application of internal combustion to transportation was waiting on the development of lightweight gasoline engines. Samuel Langley, secretary of the Smithsonian Institution, had worked for some time on aerodynamic theory. In 1896 he had built and flown a steam-driven model of a "heavier-than-air machine" with a 14-foot wing span. In 1901 he was constructing a man-carrying version, gasoline-powered, financed by a $50,000 War Department grant. Meanwhile, two brothers named Wright from Dayton, Ohio—bicycle makers by trade—were soaring in gliders at a wind-swept beach in North Carolina.

Langley had his machine ready in 1903. Twice, on October 8 and December 8, he tried launching it from a houseboat on the Potomac River. Both times mechanical snags plunged his craft into the water. Nine days after Langley's second trial, the Wrights at Kitty Hawk achieved the first manned, powered, sustained, controlled flight in history. A new sound was added to the noises of the new century—the drone of engines overhead.

Entitled "Radium," this drawing of Pierre and Marie Curie appeared in the fashionable magazine "Vanity Fair" in 1904. The year before, the couple had shared in a Nobel Prize for discovering the radioactive substance which was to revolutionize science. It was the first time a woman had been so honored, and the Curies were so lionized that their work suffered.

For the 20th Century American, there would be new sights as well as sounds. On an April night in 1896 the audience at a variety theater in New York sat in front of a 20-foot-square white screen. As the house grew dark, Thomas A. Edison waited as a young man fiddled with switches at an odd-looking contrivance dubbed the "vitascope." Suddenly, on the screen, life-sized young women danced, breakers foamed on a beach and two comedians burlesqued a boxing match. The movie industry had been born. Soon movies were the feature attraction at penny arcades and peep shows. In 1905 exhibitors would rent stores, equip them with seats, offer continuous showings for five cents, and the nickelodeon would have made its debut.

A longer time would be required before ordinary Americans would have personal knowledge of another invention of the '90s. In 1895 Guglielmo Marconi impressed signals in Morse code on "electric waves" which traveled through space. Thus was wireless telegraphy introduced to the world, a gift from the old century to the coming one. Its close relative—radiotelephony—would revolutionize home entertainment.

Americans in 1901 could literally see part of the shape of the future in the automobile, or even the earliest, flickering movies. But few had any inkling of the future significance to them of the first Nobel Prize in physics, awarded in 1901 to Wilhelm Röntgen for his discovery of X-rays in 1895. Nor, for that matter, could many realize the world importance of the 1903 prize, shared by Henri Becquerel and Pierre and Marie Curie for their work in the '90s on a peculiar phenomenon—something called "spontaneous radioactivity"—of certain substances such as uranium and radium. It would be questionable, too, if one American in a million knew of the appearance in 1900 of a book in German by a Dr. Sigmund Freud of Vienna, entitled *The Interpretation of Dreams*. To most Americans, Europe was a place to be visited if you were wealthy, ignored if you were not.

It was a relatively small number of Americans, too, who followed the factional warfare among the various groups comprising socialism in the United States. Some of these socialists voted for the former Pullman striker, Eugene V. Debs, when he ran for President on the Social Democratic party ticket in 1900. More may have been taking note when numerous Debs adherents allied with some (but by no means all) other left-wing factions and assumed the name of the Socialist Party of America in 1901. But even those who thought and voted Socialist probably had little conception of the nature of the worldwide movement of which American socialism formed a part—or what consequences that movement would soon have in Europe.

Americans, by and large, did not have their ears attuned to the sounds of the political future. Other noises stood for modernity to them—for one, the ring of the telephone bell. By 1902 there were 2,371,000 phones, about one for every 35 Americans. Streetcars were whining as they got up speed along 22,000 miles of electrified trackage. And typewriters were clicking in offices, where more and more girls in shirtwaists and leg-of-mutton sleeves appeared among the eyeshaded male bookkeepers.

In the countryside the noise might be different—the morning milk train, picking up the loads of produce for the city and dropping off the big-town newspapers, or the whistle of the mailman on a rural-free-delivery route (established 1896). It would be another few years yet until the chugging of a gasoline engine powering a tractor or a generator would be a familiar sound to a farmer. In some places it would take a generation.

The 20th Century was the cry of "Extra!" as a 40-page paper, illustrated with photographs, hit the streets. In Cleveland in 1901 the news of the year was the election as mayor of Democrat Tom Johnson, a streetcar magnate converted to progressive views, who had run on a platform of the single tax, the three-cent streetcar fare and home rule for the city. In enlarged New York City, another political maverick, Seth Low, scion of an old New York family of China traders and onetime president of Columbia University, was elected mayor to develop the civil-service system of the city and push on with subway construction.

Samuel Pierpont Langley, an eminent scientist, pioneered research in solar radiation and in heavier-than-air flying machines. He failed in his attempts to launch a gasoline-powered plane off a boat in the Potomac (below). Days later, the Wright brothers—two inspired bicycle makers from Dayton, Ohio—successfully flew a plane at a Kitty Hawk, North Carolina, beach.

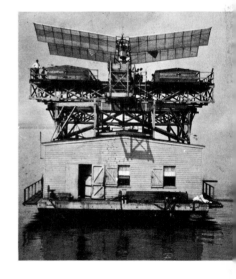

BUT in New Orleans, queen of the Mississippi delta, there was something going on as characteristically modern in its own way as efficient municipal administration. It was a music played by small bands, led by men like King Oliver and Buddy Bolden. It had elements of West Indian voodoo and African music, of revival hymns and plantation spirituals, of ragtime (just coming into vogue) and the black man's work songs and blues, the white man's folk tunes and street cries. It laughed and cried at the sadness and funniness of the world; it knew no rules, no order, none of the "culture" so carefully guarded by genteel editors and schoolmasters. It was loose and American and sassy: it came to be called jazz.

Jazz was a breaking down of accepted musical rules, and soon after 1901 a good many other rules would begin to crumble. Generally speaking, however, the mood of 1901 was one of confidence and optimism. The middle class

In 1901, a few weeks after the United States Steel Corporation was formed, "Harper's Weekly" ran this cartoon, captioned "A Steel Cinch on the World." The reference to the organization's powerful position was close to the truth, for at the time U.S. Steel was the largest business firm in history; its creation aroused alarmed outcries from the enemies of the trusts.

regarded its customs as sacred, enduring and successful. Times were good, business reviving, exports increasing, farm prices up. True, neither the prosperity nor the general sense of well-being was evenly spread.

The new century did not look quite so lustrous to the immigrant children— many not even in their teens—who toiled 10 to 12 hours a day in the coal mines as "breaker boys," picking out slate at 35 cents a day. It was no herald of deliverance to the Southern white tenant farmer with his miserably low income. It was even less promising to the Southern black, finally disfranchised in the wake of the alliance of agrarian leaders and conservatives. Not only was the Negro disfranchised, he was Jim-Crowed as well, with the blessing of the United States Supreme Court (in the Civil Rights Cases of 1883, *Plessy* v. *Ferguson* in 1896, and in other proceedings). The existence of the 14th Amendment, it seemed, still did not prevent the creation of a second-class citizenship for the black man.

Yet the woes of such as these did not stop the general buoyancy. And that buoyancy was displayed in yet another one of the nation's great fairs—this time, the Pan American Exposition of 1901, in Buffalo. To mark the significance of the exposition, President McKinley consented to deliver a speech on September 5 and to hold a public reception on September 6. The managers were certain those would be two days to remember.

THE President himself was in a mood to warm to the occasion. The triumph of the 1900 election was still fresh, and it had been topped in May of 1901 when the Supreme Court more or less ratified the acquisition of an overseas empire. Anti-imperialists had been claiming, with some relish, that the Constitution followed the flag; that Hawaii, Puerto Rico, the Philippines and our other new dependencies had acquired the same privileges that prevailed in the continental United States.

In the so-called Insular Cases the Supreme Court now set up two categories of dependencies: incorporated and unincorporated. Only the incorporated territories, it was held, were subject to the provisions of the Constitution and might expect to become part of the Union. In effect the task of spelling out the precise position and rights of America's new territories was left to Congress. If the decision was a bit tortuous, it confirmed the mandate for empire given in the preceding November, and "Mr. Dooley" shrewdly observed that whether or not the Constitution followed the flag, "th' Supreme Coort follows th' iliction returns."

Empire and prosperity thus seemed alike assured. On September 5, after the military parades along the Triumphal Causeway, President McKinley spoke feelingly to perhaps 50,000 people packed into the Esplanade and the Court of Fountains. Though long identified with the protective tariff, he said a kind word for reciprocity and enlarged trade. "Isolation is no longer possible or desirable," he noted. "The period of exclusiveness is past." He finished his talk amidst ovations.

The next afternoon, at four, he took his place in the Temple of Music for a public reception before his departure. Among the people lined up for the Presidential handshake was a dark, intense 28-year-old man named Leon Czolgosz. The son of a Polish immigrant, he had grown up in near-poverty in small Michigan towns and worked in a Cleveland wiremill. He spent long periods of unemployment in his parents' home, brooding over the doctrines of those anarchists who held that the first step in liberating the workers from the tyranny of the state must be to destroy the state's rulers.

In September of 1901 Czolgosz was in Buffalo. He had a chance to step up to within inches of the President—and his aimless life suddenly came to a focus. His hates crystallized. He brought a .32 caliber revolver, wrapped it in a handkerchief in his big palm and took his place in line. At 4:07 p.m. he fired two shots into the man standing in front of him with hand outstretched. McKinley had always been a gentle man, even as a soldier. His dazed eyes took in the scene as Czolgosz was knocked down and dragged away. "Don't let them hurt him," he said.

McKinley was rushed in a motorized ambulance to an emergency operating room on the fairgrounds. It was a touch of modernity, but the physicians did not go far enough in following medical progress. One bullet had probably been deflected by a button but surgeons did not know where the other had lodged. They did not dare probe the weakened patient's large abdomen. An X-ray machine was on display at the exposition, but was not used. The doctors sewed up the President and took him to a private home in Buffalo, where he rallied and appeared to be recovering.

The country breathed easier and was horrified over the infamy of Czolgosz (who was electrocuted within eight weeks). The doctors even told Vice President Roosevelt, who had hurried to Buffalo, that he could indulge in an Adirondack vacation. The doctors were wrong. The bullet had injured one of McKinley's kidneys and destroyed part of his pancreas. Gangrene was invading his tissues. On the 13th the President collapsed and sank into a coma for a few hours. When he came to, the end was near.

On Friday afternoon the 13th, Roosevelt was descending the slopes of Mount Marcy which he had climbed with a party of friends. He paused for lunch at a brookside. A messenger came panting up the trail bearing a message: "The President appears to be dying." Roosevelt returned to his base camp, awaiting further word. At 11 that evening he was told to hurry to the little railroad depot at North Creek to take a special train for Buffalo. He got into a lurching buckboard, and relays of horses carried him through the night. At 5:30 the next morning he reached North Creek. While he was being jounced in his buckboard, at 2:15 a.m., he had become President in fact, though the formality of oath-taking would wait a while.

Cartoonist Homer Davenport published this prophetic drawing entitled "Passing of the Horse" in the New York "Journal" in 1899. At that time people laughed at the notion that an evil-smelling and noisy automobile could nudge the uncomplaining, oat-burning horse off the roads, for few were aware of what a man named Henry Ford was quietly developing in Detroit.

M CKINLEY had presided over the transition of the United States to a nation frankly committed to industrialism and worldwide expansion, but he was not to see the transition through. His generation had passed. It was almost exactly 24 years and 6 months since Rutherford B. Hayes (in whose regiment William McKinley served) had also become President in the middle of the night, though by act of Congress rather than an assassin. That episode, too, had marked the passing of an era. It had been nearly a quarter-century of trusts and strikes, factories and dynamos, a new West and new South, urban sprawl and immigrant influx, Darwin and Fiske, Mark Twain and Bryan, D. L. Moody and John Peter Altgeld, Haymarket and Columbian Exposition. A quarter of a century that had seen the United States emerge from Civil War and Reconstruction and turn itself into a grown-up country, for weal or woe. Theodore Roosevelt boarded the train at North Creek and prepared to lead his countrymen into the 20th Century.

Railroading in its golden age

IN 1883 the railroads instituted standard time to reduce the confusions and collisions caused by the multiplicity of local time zones. An Indianapolis newspaper sarcastically commented: "The sun is no longer boss of the job. People—55,000,000 of them—must eat, sleep and work as well as travel by railroad time." Through the '80s, as rail-building continued to rise, so did complaints. It was said that the roads charged farmers ruinous freight rates, exploited their own workers and engaged in many other unscrupulous practices.

But neither the attacks on the roads, nor the vital role of rails in America's explosive growth from an agrarian to an industrial society, had any real influence on the public's attitude toward railroading. Plainly, Americans were enamored of the great puffing locomotives, enthralled by their ever-increasing speeds, delighted by the garish new luxuries of rail travel, fascinated by the trainmen's jobs. The brave engineer was a favorite hero of sentimental plays, poems and ballads. Even the postal clerk, tediously sorting the mail in transit, aroused deep interest. News of a train wreck or train robbery was a stop press item in any city room. Colorful railroad expressions like "highballing" (making a fast run) passed into common usage, and the railroads' concern over being "on" time and "making" time became part and parcel of modern living. By 1900 the people took for granted many new rail services of far-reaching consequences *(below)*, but they still were awed by the railroading spectacle.

DELIVERING COMMUTERS, trains stand six abreast at Chicago's Randolph Street Station in 1895. By then swift commuting by rail was greatly accelerating the growth of big-city suburbs.

CARRYING THE MAILS, a special express *(opposite)* is proudly contrasted with its precursor in a lithograph of the 1870s. The *Fast Mail* made its New York-Chicago run in only 24 hours.

THE MAIL CARRIER OF 100 YEARS AGO.

The FLIGHT of the FAST MAIL on the
LAKE SHORE AND MICHIGAN SOUTHERN RY.

ACCIDENTS!

NYC&HR.RR
CABOOSE
1087 E.D

SON RIVER R.R.
AD IN THE WORLD.

CHICAGO & ALTON R.R

THE GREAT
PALACE RECLINING-CHAIR ROUTE
CHICAGO AND KANSAS CITY
Between CHICAGO AND ST. LOUIS AND
ST. LOUIS AND KANSAS CITY
FREE OF EXTRA CHARGE AND WITHOUT CHANGE

PALACE DINING CARS

PULLMAN PALACE Buffet & Sleeping CARS

A LANGUID LADY promotes the advanced accommodations of a Midwestern railroad. Outlined in her chair is the route of the road.

Consolidating local roads into vast rail nets

The four-track railway advertised in the poster at left was an early landmark in the age of railroad empire building. Its creator, Cornelius Vanderbilt, invaded the field in 1862. A shrewd stock manipulator, he took over two New York lines, thereby gaining control of all direct rail traffic into and out of Manhattan island. In 1867 he broke off service between his road and the New York Central. Deprived of access to the city, the Central soon fell into Vanderbilt's hands. After building Grand Central Station for his New York terminal, he four-tracked his line between Buffalo and Albany, giving passenger trains and freights their own tracks both ways. Then his empire went on to gobble up several other major roads.

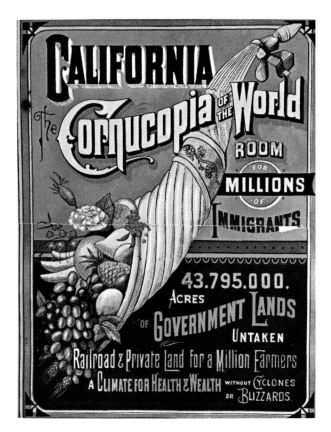

SOLICITING SETTLERS, a circular extols California's climate and its land opportunities. The influx of railborne emigrants helped triple the state's population between 1870 and 1900.

Transforming empty lands into vital commonwealths

BY 1871 the U.S. had granted more than 180 million public acres to 80-odd railroads to stimulate the building of new lines. Several roads plunged into real estate promotion to find buyers for their surplus acreage and customers for their services. Their land agents buttonholed immigrants on East Coast docks and even went abroad to recruit more. The newcomers, along with native land-seekers, were herded into crude, comfortless "Zulu cars" (below). On their arduous journey west they lived on groceries sold car-to-car by raucous vendors. They were often sidetracked for scheduled trains and delayed by washouts or snowstorms (opposite). Then, sometimes after weeks of travel, they were rudely dumped at their destination—an empty prairie.

But between 1870 and 1900 the railroads' colonizing work paid handsome dividends for the companies and the nation. In 11 Western states the population jumped from less than six million to about 17 million, while the West's rails increased from 12,000 miles to 87,000 miles.

Rolling toward new homes in the West, immigrants in their European dress while away the long hours aboard a "modern ship of the plains."

SNOWBOUND PASSENGERS turn out to clear drifts ahead of their steam engine with its great balloon stack. Wintertime runs across the Rockies and the Pacific coastal ranges were often held up by blizzards and avalanches that closed the narrow passes. In the 1870s marooned passengers suffered as long as three weeks in temperatures down to 30° below zero.

New comforts and luxuries to lure the traveler

U NTIL 1870, long train trips were a grueling experience avoided by all save immigrants and business travelers. But in the next decade, as sleeping cars and dining cars increased in number, even genteel folk ventured forth to see the country. George Pullman, the leading exponent of these special cars, devoted as much attention to their niceties as he did to crushing and absorbing all his competitors. His shiny lavatories were little wonders. His dining cars offered not only fine food but also safety from the melees at station-stop lunchrooms *(right)*. For his sleeping cars *(below)*, Pullman insisted on clean linen each night. But to save undue wear and tear on the sheets, porters had to post signs asking, "Please Take Off Your Boots Before Retiring."

TURNING IN, Pullman passengers in 1876 move freely in the carpeted aisle between the plush chair-beds. Pullman's first sleeper was tested on the Chicago & Alton in 1858.

A PULLMAN CAR of the 1870s is shown in cross section. The facing chairs at left formed lower berths; uppers folded down above. At right were a closet and two staterooms.

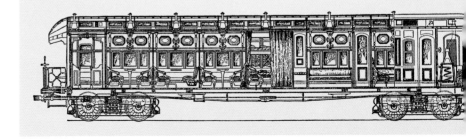

EATING IN HASTE, passengers besiege a station lunch counter during the 10-minute train stop in the 1880s. Poor food at vexing prices was the traveler's lot until the spread of dining cars and restaurant chains.

DINING AT LEISURE, well-to-do travelers enjoy six-course meals along the way. Many East Coast trains carried dining cars by the 1880s. Their menus often boasted oysters, lobster, partridge, steak and fine wines.

Symbolic figures decorate an engineers' membership certificate. This railroad union of "brothers of the footboard" was formed in 1863.

Baggagemen, switchmen and signalmen clear the night trains through in 1885. Jobs had been specialized but veterans could do several well.

The perils of railroad work in the link-and-pin days

BEHIND its glamor and excitement, railroading was a dangerous occupation. Spectacular wrecks were all too often caused by shoddy equipment, faulty roadbeds and the lag in safety apparatus. Then too, each of the many specialized railroad jobs *(above)* had its own peculiar routine hazards. Brakemen, for example, risked falling under the wheels as they applied brakes by hand for each stop *(left)*. They also lost fingers and arms as they manipulated the link-and-pin device that coupled cars. The heavy toll of accidents so increased the cost of insurance for trainmen that the "Big Four" railroad brotherhoods (membership in the first one was attested to by the certificate shown opposite) were formed—not as unions to bargain with employers but as mutual societies to reduce insurance premiums for their members.

ATOP A BOXCAR, a brakeman sets his brakes at a whistle signal from the engineer. Brakemen were rescued from their risky perches by an 1893 law requiring air brakes.

165

Century's end:
the high autumn
of railroading

A stirring sight as it rushes across the autumn landscape of Pennsylvania, the East Broad Top train at the right recaptures the zest and drama of railroading at the turn of the century. Its steam engine, noisy and angular, exerts an appeal unmatched by the sleek silent diesels that superseded it. The last car in the train, a private car reportedly used by President Grover Cleveland, expressed in fine woods and fabrics the opulence of the times.

In 1900 railroading was still in its golden age. Railroad mileage would continue to increase until 1916, then begin its long, steady decline. But by the turn of the century the railroads had finished their greatest work. In less than three decades they had sped to completion the epic westward surge that settled and closed the American frontier.

CHRONOLOGY *A timetable of American and world events: 1890-1901*

WORLD EVENTS	EXPANSION and EXPLORATION	POLITICS	MILITARY and FOREIGN AFFAIRS	ECONOMICS and SCIENCE	THOUGHT and CULTURE
1890 Mascagni's opera *Cavalleria Rusticana* completed 1890-97 Armenian revolts against Turkish rule 1890-98 Liberal labor legislation in New Zealand 1890-1948 Wilhelmina Queen of the Netherlands 1891 Franco-Russian Alliance signed 1891 Formation of the militantly nationalist and anti-Semitic Pan-German League 1891 Ibsen's *Hedda Gabler* completed 1891 Liberal Papal encyclical on labor, *Rerum Novarum*, promulgated 1891-1901 Construction of the Trans-Siberian Railway	1890 Census shows 62,947,714 inhabitants 1890 Sioux lands previously ceded to U.S. opened to settlement 1890 Oklahoma Territory organized 1891 Creation of office of Superintendent of Immigration 1891-1900 3,687,564 immigrants arrive 1891 Forest Reserve Act 1891 900,000 acres of Oklahoma land opened to settlement 1891 Immigration law bars paupers and polygamists	1890 William Jennings Bryan wins his first elective office as Congressman from Nebraska 1891 Agrarian parties agree to coalesce 1891 Creation of Circuit Courts of Appeal	1890 Authorization of reciprocal tariff arrangements by executive agreement 1890-1899 Tripartite protectorate (U.S., Germany and Britain) over Samoa	1890 onward U.S. leads Great Britain in pig-iron production 1891 W. L. Judson patents crude zipper fastener 1891 Discovery of abrasive carborundum 1891 American Sugar Refining Company achieves monopoly 1891 Edison patents motion-picture camera 1891-1900 Increasing trend toward consolidation in railroads, utilities and industry	1890 Jacob Riis's *How the Other Half Lives* published 1890 William James's *Principles of Psychology* published 1891 Carnegie Hall opened in New York 1891 Dr. Naismith invents basketball 1891 First stage appearance of George M. Cohan 1891 Hamlin Garland's *Main-Travelled Roads* published

1892   The Rise of Populism

WORLD EVENTS	EXPANSION and EXPLORATION	POLITICS	MILITARY and FOREIGN AFFAIRS	ECONOMICS and SCIENCE	THOUGHT and CULTURE
1892 Leoncavallo's *Pagliacci* completed 1893 French assume protectorates in Laos and Dahomey 1893 Opening of the Corinth Canal in Greece 1893 Tchaikovsky's *Symphonie Pathétique* completed 1893-96 Nansen Arctic expedition drifts in ice pack from Siberia to Norway	1892 Renewal of Chinese Exclusion Act 1892 Cheyenne-Arapaho and Crow reservations opened to settlement 1892-1909 Peary explores the Arctic; claims to have reached the North Pole 1892-1954 Ellis Island in New York harbor processes millions of immigrants 1893 Cherokee Strip in Oklahoma opened to settlement	1892 People's party (Populists) organized on national basis; demands free silver and a full program of reforms 1892 First national use of Australian ballot, insuring secrecy and ability to split ticket 1892 Grover Cleveland elected President; Populists win 22 electoral and one million popular votes 1893 Repeal of Sherman Silver Purchase Act splits Democratic party 1893 Supreme Court upholds constitutionality of Chinese Exclusion Act 1893 Colorado adopts female suffrage 1893 Cleveland calls extra session of Congress to study economic crisis	1892 U.S. pays indemnity to families of Italians murdered in New Orleans riots 1892-93 Bering Sea dispute with England settled by mixed international tribunal 1893 Thomas Bayard first U.S. envoy with ambassadorial rank 1893 Americans in Hawaii aided by U.S. minister in revolt against the monarchy 1893 Cleveland rebuffs movement for annexation of Hawaii 1893 First agreement with Canada for surveillance of illegal immigrants	1892 *A Manual of Bacteriology*, by G. M. Sternberg, first comprehensive work on subject published in U.S. 1892 Tesla develops alternating-current electric motor 1892 Duryea brothers produce their first automobile 1892 Homestead strike 1892 Henry Villard and J. P. Morgan organize the General Electric Company 1893 Bell loses telephone monopoly 1893 Ford builds his first auto 1893 Johns Hopkins University's Medical School founded 1893 Debs forms American Railway Union on industrial-union basis 1893-97 Panic and economic depression	1892 University of Chicago opens 1892 Formation of American Fine Arts Society 1892 "Higher Criticism" of the Bible results in heresy trials 1892 John Philip Sousa forms concert band 1893 World's Columbian Exposition in Chicago 1893 Frank Lloyd Wright completes first house as an independent architect 1893 First U.S. appearances of singers Nellie Melba and Emma Calve, and actress Eleonora Duse 1893 World Premiere of Dvorak's *New World Symphony* in New York

1894   Hard Times and the Demand for Free Silver

WORLD EVENTS	EXPANSION and EXPLORATION	POLITICS	MILITARY and FOREIGN AFFAIRS	ECONOMICS and SCIENCE	THOUGHT and CULTURE
1894 President Carnot of France assassinated 1894 Discovery of Transvaal gold fields in South Africa 1894 Dr. Sun Yat-sen forms first Chinese revolutionary society 1894-1906 Dreyfus Affair in France 1894-1917 Nicholas II Czar of Russia 1895 Germany opens	1894 Bureau of Immigration created 1894 Organization of Immigration Restriction League 1894 National Municipal League founded 1894 Carey Act authorizes public grants to states to encourage irrigation projects 1895 200 Georgia Negroes emigrate to Liberia	1894 March on Washington by "Coxey's Army" 1894 Cleveland vetoes Bland Bill for coinage of silver 1894 Populists poll almost 1.5 million votes 1894 Repercussions of Pullman strike bring Debs, Altgeld and Darrow to national prominence 1894 Labor Day declared legal holiday 1895 Silver wing of Democratic party repudiates Cleveland	1894 U.S. recognizes the Republic of Hawaii 1894 Brazilian revolutionists fire on U.S. flag	1894 American Federation of Labor formally repudiates socialism 1894 J. P. Morgan organizes Southern Railroad Company 1894 Pullman strike brings Federal intervention 1894-95 Widespread unemployment in U.S. 1895 National Association of Manufacturers organized 1895 Westinghouse constructs power generators at Niagara	1894 Charles Lawler's "Sidewalks of New York" published 1894 Formation of U.S. Golf Association 1894 Henry D. Lloyd's *Wealth Against Commonwealth*, William Harvey's *Coin's Financial School* and William Dean Howells' *A Traveller from Altruria* published 1894-95 Peak strength of anti-Catholic American Protective Association

1895 European powers intervene in peace conference ending Sino-Japanese War
1895 Röntgen discovers X-rays
1895 Marconi invents the wireless telegraph
1895 Yeats's *Poems* published
1896 Ethiopians defeat Italians at Adowa
1896 Puccini completes *La Bohème*
1896 onward Revival of Olympic Games
1897 Diamond Jubilee of Queen Victoria celebrates 60th year of her reign
1897 Greco-Turkish War
1897 British women's suffrage societies unite
1897 Rostand's *Cyrano de Bergerac* published

1898 America Becomes an Empire

1898 Port Arthur and Kiaochow leased from China by Russia and Germany respectively
1898 Pierre and Marie Curie discover radium
1898 Germany begins fleet expansion
1898 Fashoda Incident in East Africa creates Franco-British tension
1898 Kitchener defeats Dervishes at Omdurman in the Sudan
1898 Italian peasants riot against martial law and high prices
1898 Zeppelin invents rigid airship
1899 First Hague Peace Conference
1899 Germany secures Baghdad railway concession
1899-1902 Boer War
1900 Boxer Rebellion in China
1900 Puccini completes *La Tosca*
1900 Britain annexes Transvaal and Orange Free State
1900 Conrad's *Lord Jim* published
1900-46 Victor Emmanuel III king of Italy
1901 First overseas wireless communication
1901 Thomas Mann's *Buddenbrooks* published
1901-10 Edward VII king of England

1895 Treasury negotiates $62 million bond deal with Morgan and Belmont
1895 Utah adopts female suffrage
1895 Supreme Court decision in the Knight case weakens Sherman Antitrust Act
1895-1911 Republicans control both houses of Congress
1896 Silver Republicans bolt Republican convention and nominate Bryan
1896 Gold Democrats bolt convention and organize separate ticket
1896 After "Cross of Gold" speech Bryan wins Democratic nomination; Populists also nominate him
1896 Supreme Court, in *Plessy vs. Ferguson*, establishes "separate but equal" doctrine, thus legalizing segregation
1896 William McKinley elected President
1897 Dingley Tariff raises average rates to 52 per cent
1897 Supreme Court denies Interstate Commerce Commission rate-fixing power

1896 Utah statehood
1896 Rural Free Delivery inaugurated
1897 21 million acres put into forest reserves
1897-98 Gold Rush in the Klondike

1898 Louisiana disfranchises Negroes under "grandfather clause"
1898 Erdman Act authorizes government mediation in labor disputes involving interstate commerce
1898 Theodore Roosevelt elected governor of New York
1899 Organization of Anti-Imperialist League
1899 Congress authorizes use of voting machines in Federal elections

1898 Annexation of Hawaii
1898 Greater New York City chartered, incorporating Manhattan, Brooklyn, Queens, Bronx, Richmond
1898 Spain cedes Puerto Rico, Guam and the Philippines to U.S. for $20 million
1899 American Samoa organized under naval rule
1899 Isthmian Canal Commission created
1899 U.S. formally occupies Wake Island

1900 Hawaii granted territorial status
1900 Foraker Act provides for civil government in Puerto Rico
1900 Census shows 75,994,575 inhabitants
1901 Supreme Court decisions in the Insular Cases
1901 Philippines granted civil government
1901 Members of the Five Civilized Indian Tribes of the Southeast granted U.S. citizenship

1900 U.S. goes on gold standard
1900 Minneapolis holds first direct primary
1900 McKinley re-elected President
1901 McKinley assassinated; succeeded by Vice President Theodore Roosevelt
1901 Socialist Party of America organized

Feb. 1898 De Lôme letter and *Maine* disaster heighten U.S.-Spanish tensions
April 25, 1898 Congress declares war on Spain
May 1, 1898 Battle of Manila Bay
July 1, 1898 Battles of El Caney and San Juan Hill
July 3, 1898 Spanish fleet defeated at Santiago
Dec. 10, 1898 Signing of Peace of Paris ending Spanish-American War
1899 U.S. participation in First Hague Peace Conference
1899 Samoan Islands partitioned by U.S. and Germany
1899-1900 Secretary of State Hay's "circular note" to world powers results in "Open Door" policy in China
1899-1902 Filipinos revolt against American rule
1900 U.S. troops help relieve Peking during Boxer uprising
1900 General A. MacArthur offers amnesty to Filipino insurgents
1901 Emilio Aguinaldo, Filipino rebel leader, captured
1901 Army reorganization begins with opening of Army War College
1901 U.S. reluctantly accepts $24.5 million indemnity for Boxer damage and devotes half of it to a fund for Chinese students in U.S.
1901 Platt Amendment gives U.S. right to intervene in Cuban foreign and domestic policies
1901 Second Hay-Pauncefote Treaty gives U.S. free hand in Isthmian canal

---

1898 Federal Bankruptcy Act eases bankruptcy terms
1898 First U.S. forestry school opens
1898 Discovery of the ninth satellite of Saturn
1899 Standard Oil of New Jersey formed as holding company
1899 First use of spinal anesthesia
1899 Formation of National Consumers' League

1900 International Ladies Garment Workers Union formed
1900 Annual cigarette production reaches four billion
1900 Wright Brothers build their first full-scale glider
1900 R. E. Olds initiates manufacture of autos assembled from parts made by other companies
1901 Yellow Fever Commission discovers manner of transmission of the disease
1901 Carnegie retires from business to pursue philanthropy
1901 Oil discovered in Texas
1901 The U.S. Steel Corporation organized

1895 Daniel Palmer founds chiropractics

to broad construction of Monroe Doctrine
1896 British accede to U.S. demands for arbitration of Venezuela dispute
1896 Congress grants belligerent rights to Cuban rebels
1896-98 Hearst-Pulitzer "Yellow Press" rivalry fans U.S. sympathy for Cuban rebels
1897 Spain, under U.S. pressure, recalls General Weyler from Cuba and makes other concessions
1897-98 President McKinley negotiates Hawaiian annexation treaty

1896 First use of X-rays in cancer treatment
1896 William S. Hadaway patents electric stove
1896 First public exhibition of motion pictures projected on a screen
1897 Boston opens first American subway
1897 Coal miners strike in Pennsylvania, Ohio, West Virginia

1895 Stephen Crane's *Red Badge of Courage* published
1895 American Bowling Congress formed
1896 Dorothy Dix begins first popular lovelorn column
1896 "The Yellow Kid," forerunner of comic strips, appears
1896 F. P. Dunne introduces "Mr. Dooley"
1896 Billy Sunday begins evangelistic career
1897 Lester Ward's *Outlines of Sociology* published
1897 Edwin Arlington Robinson's verses, *The Children of the Night*, published
1897 Charles M. Sheldon's *In His Steps* published
1897 Library of Congress completed
1897 *Jewish Daily Forward*, leading Yiddish newspaper in U.S., founded
1897-1911 Construction of New York Public Library

1898 National Institute of Arts and Letters established
1898 "The Rosary" composed by Rogers and Nevin
1898 First exhibition of American Impressionist painters
1899 Scott Joplin's "Maple Leaf Rag" introduces ragtime to white audiences
1899 Gideon Bible Society organized
1899 Edwin Markham's poem "Man With the Hoe" published
1899 John Dewey's *The School and Society* published
1899 Thorstein Veblen's *Theory of the Leisure Class* published
1899 Hall of Fame founded as memorial to great Americans

1900 Theodore Dreiser's novel *Sister Carrie* withdrawn from sale by publisher
1900 Carry Nation inaugurates her anti-saloon career
1900 Death and immortalization of Casey Jones
1900 U.S. tennis team wins first Davis Cup tournament
1900 American Baseball League replaces defunct American Association
1901 Pan-American Exposition at Buffalo

FOR FURTHER READING

These books were selected for their interest and authority in the preparation of this volume, and for their usefulness to readers seeking additional information on specific points. An asterisk (*) marks works available in both hard-cover and paperback editions.

GENERAL READING

Bailey, Thomas A., *A Diplomatic History of the American People*. Appleton-Century-Crofts, 1958.
*Binkley, Wilfred E., *American Political Parties*. Alfred A. Knopf, 1963.
*Bryce, James, *The American Commonwealth*. G. P. Putnam's Sons, 1959.
Carman, Harry J., Harold C. Syrett and Bernard Wishy, *A History of the American People* (Vol. II). Alfred A. Knopf, 1961.
Dulles, Foster Rhea, *America Learns to Play: A History of Popular Recreation, 1607-1940*. Peter Smith, 1952.
Faulkner, Harold U., *The Decline of Laissez-Faire, 1897-1917* (Vol. VII of the Economic History of the United States Series). Holt, Rinehart & Winston, 1951. *Politics, Reform and Expansion, 1890-1900*. Harper & Row, 1959.
*Hofstadter, Richard, *The Age of Reform*. Alfred A. Knopf, 1955.
Josephson, Matthew, *The Politicos, 1865-1896*. Harcourt, Brace & World, 1938. *The Robber Barons*. Harcourt, Brace & World, 1934.
*Parrington, Vernon L., *Main Currents in American Thought*. Harcourt, Brace & World, 1939.
Schlesinger, Arthur M. Sr., *The Rise of the City, 1878-1898* (Vol. X of History of American Life Series). Macmillan, 1948.
Swisher, Carl B., *American Constitutional Development*. Houghton Mifflin, 1954.

AN INTELLECTUAL REVOLUTION (CHAPTER 1)

*Commager, Henry Steele, *The American Mind*. Yale University Press, 1950.
Conningham, Frederic A., *Currier & Ives Prints*. Crown Publishers, 1949.
Edman, Irwin (ed.), *John Dewey: His Contribution to the American Tradition*. Bobbs-Merrill, 1955.
*Hofstadter, Richard, *The American Political Tradition and the Men Who Made It*. Alfred A. Knopf, 1948. *Social Darwinism in American Thought*. George Braziller, 1959.
Larson, Orvin, *American Infidel: Robert G. Ingersoll*. Citadel, 1962.
Peters, Harry T., *Currier & Ives, Printmakers to the American People*. Doubleday, 1942.
Rudolph, Frederick, *The American College and University*. Alfred A. Knopf, 1962.
Weisberger, Bernard A., *They Gathered at the River*. Little, Brown, 1958.
Wish, Harvey, *Society and Thought in Modern America* (Vol. II of Society and Thought in America). McKay, 1962.

GREAT CITIES AND NEW AMERICANS (CHAPTERS 2 AND 3)

Antin, Mary, *The Promised Land*. Houghton Mifflin, 1917.
Barrett, James W., *Joseph Pulitzer and His World*. Vanguard, 1941.
*Beer, Thomas, *The Mauve Decade*. Alfred A. Knopf, 1937.
Blegen, Theodore C., *Land of Their Choice: The Immigrants Write Home*. University of Minnesota Press, 1955.
Commons, John R., and others, *History of Labour in the United States* (Vol. II). Macmillan, 1951.
Downey, Fairfax, *Portrait of an Era, As Drawn by Charles Dana Gibson*. Charles Scribner's Sons, 1936.
Faulkner, Harold U., *The Quest for Social Justice, 1898-1914* (Vol. XI of History of American Life Series). Macmillan, 1945.
Gompers, Samuel, *Seventy Years of Life and Labor*. E. P. Dutton, 1957.
Gosnell, Harold F., *Machine Politics: Chicago Model*. University of Chicago Press, 1937.
*Handlin, Oscar, *Race and Nationality in American Life*. Little, Brown, 1957. *The Uprooted*. Little, Brown, 1951.
Hansen, Marcus L., *The Immigrant in American History*. Harvard University Press, 1940.
Higham, John, *Strangers in the Land: Patterns of American Nativism, 1860-1925*. Rutgers University Press, 1955.
*Jones, Maldwyn A., *American Immigration*. University of Chicago Press, 1960.
Kouwenhoven, John A., *The Columbia Historical Portrait of New York*. Doubleday, 1953.
Morell, Parker, *Lillian Russell*. Garden City Publishing Co., 1943.

Mott, Frank L., *American Journalism: 1690-1960*. Macmillan, 1962. *A History of American Magazines* (Vols. III and IV). Harvard University Press, 1957.
*Riis, Jacob A., *How the Other Half Lives*. Peter Smith, 1959.
Seymour, Harold, *Baseball: The Early Years*. Oxford University Press, 1960.
Solomon, Barbara M., *Ancestors and Immigrants: A Changing New England Tradition*. Harvard University Press, 1956.
Steffens, Lincoln, *The Autobiography of Lincoln Steffens*. Harcourt, Brace & World, 1936.
Wecter, Dixon, *The Saga of American Society*. Charles Scribner's Sons, 1957.
Weisberger, Bernard A., *The American Newspaperman*. University of Chicago Press, 1961.
*Wittke, Carl, *We Who Built America: The Saga of the Immigrant*. Prentice-Hall, 1939.

PANIC AND A CRISIS ELECTION (CHAPTERS 4 AND 5)

*Barnard, Harry, *Eagle Forgotten: The Life of John Peter Altgeld*. Duell, Sloan & Pearce, 1948.
Buck, Solon J., *The Agrarian Crusade*. Yale University Press, 1920.
Ginger, Raymond, *The Bending Cross: A Biography of Eugene Victor Debs*. Rutgers University Press, 1949.
Glad, Paul W., *The Trumpet Soundeth: William Jennings Bryan and His Democracy, 1896-1912*. University of Nebraska Press, 1960.
Hibben, Paxton, *The Peerless Leader: William Jennings Bryan*. Farrar, Straus, 1929.
*Hicks, John D., *The Populist Revolt*. University of Minnesota Press, 1955.
Leech, Margaret K., *In the Days of McKinley*. Harper & Row, 1959.
Lindsey, Almont, *The Pullman Strike*. University of Chicago Press, 1942.
Meltzer, Milton, *Mark Twain Himself*. Thomas Y. Crowell, 1960.
Nevins, Allan, *Grover Cleveland: A Study in Courage*. Dodd, Mead, 1958.
Paine, Albert Bigelow, *Mark Twain* (2 vols.). Harper & Row, 1935.
Pierce, Bessie L. and J. L. Norris (eds.), *As Others See Chicago; Impressions of Visitors, 1673-1933*. University of Chicago Press, 1933.
Woodward, C. Vann, *Origins of the New South, 1877-1913* (Vol. IX of the History of the South Series). Louisiana State University Press, 1951. *Tom Watson, Agrarian Rebel*. Holt, Rinehart & Winston, 1955.

IMPERIAL ADVENTURE (CHAPTER 6)

Ellis, Elmer (ed.), *Mr. Dooley at His Best*. Charles Scribner's Sons, 1938.
*Freidel, Frank B., *The Splendid Little War*. Little, Brown, 1958.
Garraty, John A., *Henry Cabot Lodge*. Alfred A. Knopf, 1953.
Millis, Walter, *The Martial Spirit: A Study of Our War with Spain*. Houghton Mifflin, 1937.
Mitchell, Donald W., *History of the Modern American Navy*. Alfred A. Knopf, 1946.
*Post, Charles Johnson, *The Little War of Private Post*. Little, Brown, 1960.
Pratt, Julius W., *Expansionists of 1898*. Peter Smith, 1952.
*Pringle, Henry F., *Theodore Roosevelt*. Harcourt, Brace & World, 1939.
Swanberg, W. A., *Citizen Hearst*. Charles Scribner's Sons, 1961.

ERA OF CONFIDENCE (CHAPTER 7)

Clark, Victor S., *History of Manufactures in the United States, 1607-1928* (3 vols.). Peter Smith, 1949.
Harbaugh, William H., *Power and Responsibility: The Life and Times of Theodore Roosevelt*. Farrar, Straus, 1961.
Holbrook, Stewart H., *Machines of Plenty*. Macmillan, 1955.
Morris, Lloyd, *Not So Long Ago*. Random House, 1949.
Oliver, John W., *History of American Technology*. Ronald Press Co., 1956.
*Stover, John F., *American Railroads*. University of Chicago Press, 1961.
Wilson, Mitchell A., *American Science and Invention*. Bonanza Books, 1960.
*Woodward, C. Vann, *The Strange Career of Jim Crow*. Peter Smith, 1963.

ACKNOWLEDGMENTS

The editors of this book are particularly indebted to the following persons and institutions: David Brody, Assistant Professor of History, Columbia University; Albert K. Baragwanath and Henriette Beal, Museum of the City of New York; Paul Bride, The New-York Historical Society, New York City; Maurice R. Cheyette, New York City; Frederic A. Conningham, Sea Cliff, New York; Roy King, New York City; Raymond C. Fingado, Staten Island Historical Society, Staten Island, New York; Richard Hofstadter, DeWitt Clinton Professor of American History, Columbia University; Betty C. Moore, Research Scientist in Zoology, Columbia University; Paul Myers, Theatre Collection, New York Public Library; Sol Novin, Culver Pictures, Inc., New York City; Mary Frances Rhymer, Chicago Historical Society, Chicago; and Judy Higgins.

The author, for his part, wishes to acknowledge the assistance of Jane Hobson and Lawrence Jorgensen.

PICTURE CREDITS

CHAPTER 1:—The Metropolitan Museum of Art, Alfred N. Punnett Fund, 1939. 8 through 12—Culver. 14, 15—Bettmann except left Culver. 16, 17—Culver except right courtesy William James. 18,19—Courtesy F. A. Conningham; Herbert Orth, courtesy The Harry T. Peters Collection, Museum of the City of New York. 20,21—Herbert Orth, courtesy The Harry T. Peters Collection, Museum of the City of New York except bottom left Eric Schaal, courtesy of Roy King from his Currier & Ives Collection. 22,23—Herbert Orth, courtesy The Harry T. Peters Collection, Museum of the City of New York. 24,25—Herbert Orth, courtesy The Harry T. Peters Collection, Museum of the City of New York. 26,27—Herbert Orth, courtesy of the New York Yacht Club; Herbert Orth, courtesy The Harry T. Peters Collection, Museum of the City of New York. 28,29—Herbert Orth, courtesy The Harry T. Peters Collection, Museum of the City of New York except bottom left The Harry T. Peters Collection, Museum of the City of New York, courtesy American Heritage Publishing Co., Inc. 30,31—Herbert Orth, courtesy The Harry T. Peters Collection, Museum of the City of New York.

CHAPTER 2: 32—Arthur Siegel, courtesy Chicago Historical Society. 34, 35—Culver; Bettmann. 36, 37—Bettmann. 38—Culver. 39—By special permission of the *Ladies' Home Journal*, © 1889 The Curtis Publishing Co.—Culver—NYPL. 40, 41—Bettmann except right Culver. 42, 43—Culver; Bettmann. 44, 45—NYPL; Eric Schaal, courtesy "Gallery of Modern Art (including the Huntington Hartford Collection), New York." 46, 47—Museum of the City of New York; Brown—Culver (2). 48—Museum of the City of New York. 49—Bettmann—Culver. 50, 51—Staten Island Historical Society except left Culver—Culver (2); United Press International; photograph by Byron, The Byron Collection, Museum of the City of New York. 52—NYPL-prints division—Herbert Orth, NYPL-Theater Collection; Brown. 53—"Gallery of Modern Art (including the Huntington Hartford Collection), New York," courtesy American Heritage Publishing Co., Inc. 54,55—Museum of the City of New York, courtesy American Heritage Publishing Co., Inc.; Culver—Culver; photograph by Byron, The Byron Collection, Museum of the City of New York. 56,57—Culver except bottom left photograph by Byron, The Byron Collection, Museum of the City of New York.

CHAPTER 3: 58—Courtesy of The White House. 60—Courtesy LC. 64, 65—Bettmann. 66, 67—Courtesy Henry Cabot Lodge; Culver. 68, 69—Bettmann; graph by Lewis Zacks. 70, 71—Culver; George Eastman House Collection. 72, 73—Photograph by Jacob A. Riis, The Jacob A. Riis Collection, Museum of the City of New York except center photograph by Byron, The Byron Collection, Museum of the City of New York. 74—Bettmann—Robert Kafka, Museum of the City of New York. 75—Photograph by Jacob A. Riis, The Jacob A. Riis Collection, Museum of the City of New York. 76, 77—George Eastman House Collection except left: Bettmann—courtesy LC. 78,79—Photograph by Byron, The Byron Collection, Museum of the City of New York—Culver; photograph by Jacob A. Riis, The Jacob A. Riis Collection, Museum of the City of New York. 80,81—Bettmann.

CHAPTER 4: 82—Collection of Richard F. Cleveland, Baltimore. 84—Bettmann—Culver. 85—From the J. Doyle DeWitt Collection. 86,87—Culver. 88,89—Culver except left Bettmann. 90,91—Bettmann—Culver. 92,93—Bettmann; Culver. 94 through 98—Courtesy Chicago Historical Society. 99—Courtesy Chicago Historical Society except top right Walter W. Krutz, courtesy Chicago Historical Society. 100, 101—Courtesy Chicago Historical Society.

CHAPTER 5: 102—Culver. 104, 105—Bettmann except top right Culver. 106 through 109—Culver. 110,111—Bettmann; Culver. 113—Bettmann. 114,115—NYPL; by permission of the Trustees of the Estate of Samuel L. Clemens (Mark Twain) Deceased. 116,117—Courtesy of the Berg Collection, NYPL; by permission of the Trustees of the Estate of Samuel L. Clemens (Mark Twain) Deceased; courtesy Samuel C. Webster—Piaget, courtesy Missouri Historical Society; courtesy of the Berg Collection, NYPL. 118, 119—Brown; NYPL—Gjon Mili, courtesy U.S. Corps of Engineers, Memphis District. 120, 121—NYPL; Culver—NYPL; from *Mark Twain Himself*, by Milton Meltzer; from *Mark Twain's Sketches, New and Old*. 122—Culver. 123—Bettmann—Mark Twain Memorial, Hartford. 124, 125—United Press International except left courtesy Warner Bros. Pictures Inc.

CHAPTER 6: 126—Courtesy of the State of Vermont and American Heritage Publishing Co., Inc. 128 through 132—Culver. 133—U.S. Signal Corps photo no. 111-SC-90119 in the National Archives. 135—U.S. Signal Corps photo no. 111-B-5128 (Brady Collection) in the National Archives—U.S. Signal Corps photo no. 111-SC-90118 in the National Archives. 138, 139—U.S. Signal Corps photo no. 111-SC-85795 in the National Archives; Culver. 140—U.S. Signal Corps photo no. 111-SC-94543 in the National Archives. 141 through 147—Herbert Orth, paintings courtesy Mrs. Charles Johnson Post and Miss Phyllis B. Post.

CHAPTER 7: 148—Eric Schaal courtesy N-YHS. 150,151,152—Culver. 153—Culver—Brown. 154, 155—Bettmann. 156, 157—Copyright 1952, Witbeck Studio, Trains Collection; courtesy The W. H. Coverdale Collection and American Heritage Publishing Co., Inc. 158,159—Walter Daran, courtesy The W. H. Coverdale Collection; courtesy LC and American Heritage Publishing Co., Inc. 160—From the Bella C. Landauer Collection in the N-YHS, courtesy American Heritage Publishing Co., Inc.—Culver. 161—Museum of the City of New York. 162,163—Culver; courtesy Chicago Historical Society—NYPL; Culver. 164—From the Bella C. Landauer Collection in the N-YHS, courtesy American Heritage Publishing Co., Inc. 165—Courtesy LC and American Heritage Publishing Co., Inc.—Culver. 166,167—Farrell Grehan.

INDEX

*This symbol in front of a page number indicates a photograph or painting of the subject mentioned.

Printed in U.S.A.

XXXX